# PATHWAYS

## Listening, Speaking, and Critical Thinking

## 4A

Paul MacIntyre

NATIONAL GEOGRAPHIC LEARNING | CENGAGE Learning

Andover • Melbourne • Mexico City • Stamford, CT • Toronto • Hong Kong • New Delhi • Seoul • Singapore • Tokyo

**Pathways Split Text 4A**
**Listening, Speaking, and Critical Thinking**
Paul MacIntyre

Regional Director, Asia ELT/School:
Michael Cahill

Publisher, Asia ELT/School: Edward Yoshioka

Regional Manager, Production & Rights (Asia):
Pauline Lim

Senior Production Executive (Asia): Cindy Chai

Publisher: Sherrise Roehr

Executive Editor: Laura Le Dréan

Acquisitions Editor: Tom Jefferies

Associate Development Editor:
Marissa Petrarca

Director of Global Marketing: Ian Martin

Marketing Manager: Caitlin Driscoll

Marketing Manager: Katie Kelley

Marketing Manager: Emily Stewart

Director of Content and Media Production:
Michael Burggren

Content Project Manager: Daisy Sosa

Manufacturing Manager: Marcia Locke

Manufacturing Buyer: Marybeth Hennebury

Cover Design: Page 2 LLC

Cover Image: JIM BRANDENBURG/MINDEN
PICTURES/National Geographic Image
Collection

Interior Design: Page 2 LLC

Composition: Cenveo Publisher Services/
Nesbitt Graphics, Inc.

For product information and technology assistance, contact us at
**Cengage Learning Asia Customer Support, 65-6410-1200**
For permission to use material from this text or product,
submit all requests online at **www.cengageasia.com/permissions**
Further permissions questions can be emailed to
**asia.permissionrequest@cengage.com**

ISBN 13: 978-1-285-15978-2
ISBN 10: 1-285-15978-0

**Cengage Learning Asia Pte Ltd**
151 Lorong Chuan #02-08
New Tech Park
Singapore 556741

**National Geographic Learning**
20 Channel Center St.
Boston, MA 02210
USA

Cengage Learning is a leading provider of customized learning solutions with office locations around the globe, including Andover, Melbourne, Mexico City, Stamford (CT), Toronto, Hong Kong, New Delhi, Seoul, Singapore, and Tokyo. Locate your local office at **www.cengage.com/global**

Cengage Learning products are represented in Canada by Nelson Education, Ltd.

Visit National Geographic Learning online at **ngl.cengage.com**
For product information, visit our website at **www.cengageasia.com**

Printed in Singapore
2 3 4 5 6 7 8 17 16 15 14

*The author and publisher would like to thank the following reviewers:*

**UNITED STATES** Adrianne Aiko Thompson, Miami Dade College, Miami, Florida; **Gokhan Alkanat**, Auburn University at Montgomery, Alabama; **Nikki Ashcraft**, Shenandoah University, VA; **Karin Avila-John**, University of Dayton, Ohio; **Shirley Baker**, Alliant International University, California; **John Baker**, Oakland Community College, Michigan; **Evina Baquiran Torres**, Zoni Language Centers, New York; **Michelle Bell**, University of South Florida, Florida; **Nancy Boyer**, Golden West College, California; **Carol Brutza**, Gateway Community College, Connecticut; **Sarah Camp**, University of Kentucky, Center for ESL, Kentucky; **Maria Caratini**, Eastfield College, Texas; **Ana Maria Cepero**, Miami Dade College, Florida; **Daniel Chaboya**, Tulsa Community College, Oklahoma; **Patricia Chukwueke**, English Language Institute – UCSD Extension, California; **Julia A. Correia**, Henderson State University, Connecticut; **Suzanne Crisci**, Bunker Hill Community College, Massachusetts; **Katie Crowder**, University of North Texas, Texas; **Lynda Dalgish**, Concordia College, New York; **Jeffrey Diluglio**, Center for English Language and Orientation Programs: Boston University, Massachusetts; **Tim DiMatteo**, Southern New Hampshire University, New Hampshire; **Scott Dirks**, Kaplan International Center at Harvard Square, Massachusetts; **Margo Downey**, Center for English Language and Orientation Programs: Boston University, Massachusetts; **John Drezek**, Richland College, Texas; **Anwar El-Issa**, Antelope Valley College, California; **Anrisa Fannin**, The International Education Center at Diablo Valley College, California; **Jennie Farnell**, University of Connecticut, American Language Program, Connecticut; **Mark Fisher**, Lone Star College, Texas; **Celeste Flowers**, University of Central Arkansas, Arkansas; **John Fox**, English Language Institute, Georgia; **Pradel R. Frank**, Miami Dade College, Florida; **Sally Gearheart**, Santa Rosa Jr. College, California; **Karen Grubbs**, ELS Language Centers, Florida; **Joni Hagigeorges**, Salem State University, Massachusetts; **Valerie Heming**, University of Central Missouri, Missouri; **Mary Hill**, North Shore Community College, Massachusetts; **Harry L. Holden**, North Lake College, Texas; **Ingrid Holm**, University of Massachusetts Amherst, Massachusetts; **Marianne Hsu Santelli**, Middlesex County College, New Jersey; **Katie Hurter**, Lone Star College – North Harris, Texas; **Justin Jernigan**, Georgia Gwinnett College, Georgia; **Barbara A. Jonckheere**, American Language Institute at California State University, Long Beach, California; **Susan Jordan**, Fisher College, Massachusetts; **Maria Kasparova**, Bergen Community College, New Jersey; **Gail Kellersberger**, University of Houston-Downtown, Texas; **Christina Kelso**, Austin Peay State University, Tennessee; **Daryl Kinney**, Los Angeles City College, California; **Leslie Kosel Eckstein**, Hillsborough Community College, Florida; **Beth Kozbial Ernst**, University of Wisconsin-Eau Claire, Wisconsin; **Jennifer Lacroix**, Center for English Language and Orientation Programs: Boston University, Massachusetts; **Stuart Landers**, Missouri State University, Missouri; **Margaret V. Layton**, University of Nevada, Reno Intensive English Language Center, Nevada; **Heidi Lieb**, Bergen Community College, New Jersey; **Kerry Linder**, Language Studies International New York, New York; **Jenifer Lucas-Uygun**, Passaic County Community College, New Jersey; **Alison MacAdams**, Approach International Student Center, Massachusetts; **Craig Machado**, Norwalk Community College, Connecticut; **Andrew J. MacNeill**, Southwestern College, California; **Melanie A. Majeski**, Naugatuck Valley Community College, Connecticut; **Wendy Maloney**, College of DuPage, Illinois; **Chris Mares**, University of Maine – Intensive English Institute, Maine; **Josefina Mark**, Union County College, New Jersey; **Connie Mathews**, Nashville State Community College, Tennessee; **Bette Matthews**, Mid-Pacific Institute, Hawaii; **Marla McDaniels Heath**, Norwalk Community College, Connecticut; **Kimberly McGrath Moreira**, University of Miami, Florida; **Sara McKinnon**, College of Marin, California; **Christine Mekkaoui**, Pittsburg State University, Kansas; **Holly A. Milkowart**, Johnson County Community College, Kansas; **Warren Mosher**, University of Miami, Florida; **Lukas Murphy**, Westchester Community College, New York; **Elena Nehrebecki**, Hudson Community College, New Jersey; **Bjarne Nielsen**, Central Piedmont Community College, North Carolina; **David Nippoldt**, Reedley College, California; **Lucia Parsley**, Virginia Commonwealth University, Virginia; **Wendy Patriquin**, Parkland College, Illinois; **Marion Piccolomini**, Communicate With Ease, LTD, Pennsylvania; **Carolyn Prager**, Spanish-American Institute, New York; **Eileen Prince**, Prince Language Associates Incorporated, Massachusetts; **Sema Pulak**, Texas A & M University, Texas; **James T. Raby**, Clark University, Massachusetts; **Anouchka Rachelson**, Miami-Dade College, Florida; **Lynn Ramage Schaefer**, University of Central Arkansas, Arkansas; **Sherry Rasmussen**, DePaul University, Illinois; **Amy Renehan**, University of Washington, Washington; **Esther Robbins**, Prince George's Community College, Pennsylvania; **Helen Roland**, Miami Dade College, Florida; **Linda Roth**, Vanderbilt University English Language Center, Tennessee; **Janine Rudnick**, El Paso Community College, Texas; **Rita Rutkowski Weber**, University of Wisconsin – Milwaukee, Wisconsin; **Elena Sapp**, INTO Oregon State University, Oregon; **Margaret Shippey**, Miami Dade College, Florida; **Lisa Sieg**, Murray State University, Kentucky; **Alison Stamps**, ESL Center at Mississippi State University, Mississippi; **Peggy Street**, ELS Language Centers, Miami, Florida; **Lydia Streiter**, York College Adult Learning Center, New York; **Nicholas Taggart**, Arkansas State University, Arkansas; **Marcia Takacs**, Coastline Community College, California; **Tamara Teffeteller**, University of California Los Angeles, American Language Center, California; **Rebecca Toner**, English Language Programs, University of Pennsylvania, Pennsylvania; **William G. Trudeau**, Missouri Southern State University, Missouri; **Troy Tucker**, Edison State College, Florida; **Maria Vargas-O'Neel**, Miami Dade College, Florida; **Amerca Vazquez**, Miami Dade College, Florida; **Alison Vinande**, Modesto Junior College, California; **Christie Ward**, Intensive English Language Program, Central Connecticut State University, Connecticut; **Colin S. Ward**, Lone Star College-North Harris, Texas; **Denise L. Warner**, Lansing Community College, Michigan; **Wendy Wish-Bogue**, Valencia Community College, Florida; **Cissy Wong**, Sacramento City College, California; **Kimberly Yoder**, Kent State University, ESL Center, Ohio.

**ASIA** **Teoh Swee Ai**, Universiti Teknologi Mara, Malaysia; **Nor Azni Abdullah**, Universiti Teknologi Mara, Malaysia; **Thomas E. Bieri**, Nagoya College, Japan; **Paul Bournhonesque**, Seoul National University of Technology, Korea; **Michael C. Cheng**, National Chengchi University; **Fu-Dong Chiou**, National Taiwan University; **Derek Currie,** Korea University, Sejong Institute of Foreign Language Studies, Korea; **Christoph A. Hafner**, City University of Hong Kong, Hong Kong; **Wenhua Hsu**, I-Shou University; **Helen Huntley**, Hanoi University, Vietnam; **Rob Higgens**, Ritsumeikan University, Japan; **Shih Fan Kao**, JinWen University of Science and Technology; **Ikuko Kashiwabara**, Osaka Electro-Communication University, Japan; **Richard S. Lavin**, Prefecturla University of Kumamoto, Japan; **Mike Lay,** American Institute, Cambodia; **Byoung-Kyo Lee**, Yonsei University, Korea; **Lin Li**, Capital Normal University, China; **Hudson Murrell**, Baiko Gakuin University, Japan; **Keiichi Narita**, Niigata University, Japan; **Huynh Thi Ai Nguyen**, Vietnam USA Society, Vietnam; **James Pham**, IDP Phnom Penh, Cambodia; **Duncan Rose**, British Council, Singapore; **Simone Samuels**, The Indonesia Australia Language Foundation Jakarta, Indonesia; **Wang Songmei**, Beijing Institute of Education Faculty, China; **Chien-Wen Jenny Tseng**, National Sun Yat-Sen University; **Hajime Uematsu**, Hirosaki University, Japan

**AUSTRALIA** **Susan Austin,** University of South Australia, **Joanne Cummins**, Swinburne College; **Pamela Humphreys**, Griffith University

**LATIN AMERICA AND THE CARIBBEAN** **Ramon Aguilar**, Universidad Tecnológica de Hermosillo, México; **Livia de Araujo Donnini Rodrigues**, University of São Paolo, Brazil; **Cecilia Avila**, Universidad de Xapala, México; Beth Bartlett, Centro Cultural Colombo Americano, Cali, Colombia; **Raúl Billini**, Colegio Loyola, Dominican Republic; **Nohora Edith Bryan**, Universidad de La Sabana, Colombia; **Raquel Hernández Cantú**, Instituto Tecnológico de Monterrey, Mexico; **Millie Commander**, Inter American University of Puerto Rico, Puerto Rico; **Edwin Marín-Arroyo**, Instituto Tecnológico de Costa Rica; **Rosario Mena**, Instituto Cultural Dominico-Americano, Dominican Republic; **Elizabeth Ortiz Lozada**, COPEI-COPOL English Institute, Ecuador; **Gilberto Rios Zamora**, Sinaloa State Language Center, Mexico; **Patricia Veciños**, El Instituto Cultural Argentino Norteamericano, Argentina

**MIDDLE EAST AND NORTH AFRICA** **Tom Farkas**, American University of Cairo, Egypt; **Ghada Hozayen**, Arab Academy for Science, Technology and Maritime Transport, Egypt

| Grammar | Speaking Skills | Viewing | Critical Thinking Skills |
|---|---|---|---|
| The Passive Voice<br><br>Using an Agent in Passive Voice Sentences | Introducing a Topic<br><br>Agreeing or Disagreeing<br><br>**Student to Student:**<br>Apologizing for Interrupting<br><br>**Presentation Skills:**<br>Making Eye Contact | **Video:**<br>*Tuareg Farmers*<br><br>Viewing to Confirm Predictions<br><br>Viewing for Main Ideas | Inferring Information Not Stated in a Conversation<br><br>Understanding Visuals<br><br>Organizing Ideas for a Discussion<br><br>Using New Vocabulary in a Discussion<br><br>Using a Graphic Organizer<br><br>**Critical Thinking Focus:**<br>Identifying the Lecture Topic |
| Restrictive Adjective Clauses<br><br>Non-Restrictive Adjective Clauses | Introducing Examples<br><br>Brainstorming<br><br>Responding to and Refuting an Argument<br><br>**Student to Student:**<br>Expressing Encouragement<br><br>**Presentation Skills:**<br>Speaking with Confidence | **Video:**<br>*Crocodiles of Sri Lanka*<br><br>Note-Taking while Viewing<br><br>Using Video Information to Role-play | Expressing Individual Ideas Using New Grammar and Vocabulary<br><br>Restating Information from Notes<br><br>Understanding Visuals<br><br>Organizing Ideas for a Discussion<br><br>Expressing and Explaining Opinions<br><br>Arguing a Point of View<br><br>**Critical Thinking Focus:**<br>Evaluating Arguments in a Debate |
| Compound Adjectives<br><br>Tag Questions | Paraphrasing<br><br>Asking for Clarification<br><br>**Student to Student:**<br>Asking about Personal Opinions<br><br>**Presentation Skills:**<br>Preparing Your Notes | **Video:**<br>*Skin Mask*<br><br>Predicting Content<br><br>Viewing for Main Ideas<br><br>Sequencing Events | Expressing and Explaining Opinions about Beauty<br><br>Paraphrasing and Explaining Quotations<br><br>Creating Sentences and Using New Grammar<br><br>Discussing Survey Results<br><br>Organizing a Group Presentation<br><br>**Critical Thinking Focus:**<br>Understanding Quotations |
| The Future Perfect<br><br>The Future Perfect Progressive | Emphasizing Important Information<br><br>Expressing Approval and Disapproval<br><br>**Student to Student:**<br>Conceding a Point<br><br>**Presentation Skills:**<br>Fighting Nervousness | **Video:**<br>*Solar Power*<br><br>Viewing for Specific Information<br><br>Viewing for Main Ideas | Discussing Unit Content Using New Vocabulary<br><br>Using a Graphic Organizer to Take Notes<br><br>Understanding Visuals<br><br>Evaluating Pros and Cons of Energy Sources<br><br>Analyzing and Ranking Statements and Providing Reasons<br><br>**Critical Thinking Focus:**<br>Using an Outline to Take Notes |
| Using Past Modals to Make Guesses about the Past<br><br>Using Past Modals to Make Inferences | Expressing Surprise<br><br>Expressing Hopes<br><br>**Student to Student:**<br>Expressing Interest<br><br>**Presentation Skills:**<br>Preparing for Audience Questions | **Video:**<br>*Wildebeest Migration*<br><br>Understanding and Interpreting Visuals<br><br>Sequencing Events<br><br>Note-Taking | Making Inferences about Unit Content<br><br>Presenting Theories and Evidence about Early Humans<br><br>Using a Graphic Organizer<br><br>Understanding Visuals<br><br>Restating Information from a Listening<br><br>**Critical Thinking Focus:**<br>Understanding Scientific Theories |

Each unit consists of two lessons which include the following sections:

Building Vocabulary
Using Vocabulary
Developing Listening Skills
Exploring Spoken English
Speaking (called "Engage" in Lesson B)

An **academic pathway** is clearly labeled for learners, starting with formal listening (e.g., lectures) and moving to a more informal context (e.g., a conversation between students in a study group).

The **"Exploring the Theme"** section provides a visual introduction to the unit and encourages learners to think critically and share ideas about the unit topic.

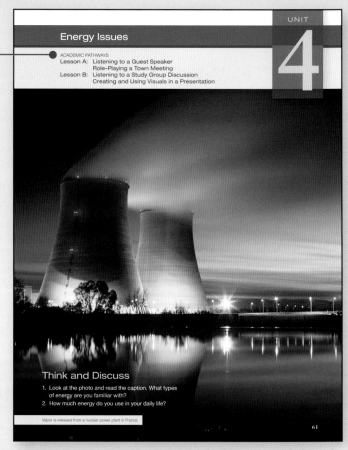

UNIT 4

Energy Issues

ACADEMIC PATHWAYS
Lesson A: Listening to a Guest Speaker
Role-Playing a Town Meeting
Lesson B: Listening to a Study Group Discussion
Creating and Using Visuals in a Presentation

**Think and Discuss**

1. Look at the photo and read the caption. What types of energy are you familiar with?
2. How much energy do you use in your daily life?

Vapor is released from a nuclear power plant in France.

61

**Exploring the Theme:**
**Energy Issues**

A | Look at the photos and read the captions. Then answer the questions.

1. How do you think energy use has changed over time?
2. In the future, do you think you will be using more or less electricity than you do now? Why do you think so?
3. Would you be willing to live next to a large energy facility such as a nuclear power plant or wind farm? Explain your answer.

Wind power provides energy to farms and homes in Abilene, Texas.

**Big Power, Big Risks**

By the year 2030, the demand for energy is expected to be double what it was in the year 2000. Providing the enormous quantity of energy the world needs is a difficult task, and there is often risk for workers, the public, and the environment.

In this village, lights shine from nearly every house. However, the world is still far away from providing inexpensive electricity. In fact, about one in four people still have no electricity at all.

**Key academic and high-frequency vocabulary**
is introduced, practiced, and expanded throughout each unit. Lessons A and B each present and practice 10 terms.

A **"Developing Listening Skills"**
section follows a before, during, and after listening approach to give learners the tools necessary to master listening skills for a variety of contexts.

**Listening activities**
encourage learners to listen for and consolidate key information, reinforcing the language, and allowing learners to think critically about the information they hear.

---

🎧 **A** | **Meaning from Context.** Read and listen to the news report about the Deepwater Horizon oil spill. Notice the words in blue. These are words you will hear and use in Lesson A.

On April 20, 2010, one of the worst oil spills in history began in the Gulf of Mexico. The spill occurred at an oil rig, called the Deepwater Horizon, which is owned by the BP company. A buildup of pressure caused natural gas to shoot up suddenly from the ocean floor. The gas **triggered** a terrible explosion and a fire on the oil rig. After the explosion, the crew **abandoned** the platform and escaped in lifeboats. Unfortunately, eleven workers were never found.

A beach in the United States is covered with oil after the Deepwater Horizon oil spill.

For weeks, no one was sure just how much oil was being **released** into the Gulf of Mexico. Gradually, information about the damage from the oil spill **emerged**. It was discovered that between 50,000 to 60,000 barrels of oil a day were flowing into the Gulf. **Experts** from BP and other organizations tried to stop the spill, but it continued for nearly three months. By the time the leak was stopped, the beautiful blue waters of the Gulf had been **contaminated** with nearly 5 million barrels of oil.

The disaster did serious harm to the fishing and tourism industries in the southern United States. Pictures of birds that had been **exposed** to the thick oil appeared daily in the news. The American public **reacted** angrily, and the spill created a huge **controversy**. Some people even wanted to stop oil companies from drilling in the Gulf of Mexico. BP set aside 20 billion dollars to **compensate** fishermen, hotel owners, and store owners whose businesses were impacted by the spill.

**B** | Match each word in blue from exercise **A** with its definition. Use your dictionary to help you.

1. triggered (v.) ____
2. abandoned (v.) ____
3. released (v.) ____
4. emerged (v.) ____
5. experts (n.) ____
6. contaminated (v.) ____
7. exposed (v.) ____
8. reacted (v.) ____
9. controversy (n.) ____
10. compensate (v.) ____

a. to pay someone to replace lost money or things
b. became known; appeared
c. responded to
d. caused an event to begin to happen
e. left a place, thing, or person permanently
f. people who are very skilled or who know a lot about a particular subject
g. entered the surrounding atmosphere or area; freed
h. a disagreement, especially about a public policy or moral issue that people feel strongly about
i. made something dirty, harmful, or dangerous because of chemicals or radiation
j. placed in a dangerous situation

---

### Before Listening

👥 **Predicting Content.** Work with a partner. Look at the map and diagram. Discuss the questions.

1. Use your dictionary and look up these terms: *containment, radiation, radioactive, half-life.* How do you predict these words will be used in the lecture?
2. Locate the containment structure in the diagram. Why do you think this structure is important? Explain your ideas.

A modern nuclear power plant

### Listening: A Guest Speaker

**Critical Thinking Focus: Using an Outline to Take Notes**

Using an outline can help you take organized and clear notes. In an outline, indicate main ideas with Roman numerals (I, II, III) and capital letters (A, B, C). Indicate details with numbers. As information becomes more specific, move it to the right.

🎧 **A** | Listen to the introduction to a lecture about the Chernobyl nuclear disaster. Read the outline as you listen.

I. Background
  A. 1970s & 1980s: Soviet Union developed nuclear technology.
  B. 1986: 25 plants w/ safety probs.
II. Chernobyl disaster
  A. Causes
    1. Mistakes during safety test
    2. No containment building to limit fire and radiation
  B. Result: explosion→people dead

👥 **B** | **Discussion.** With a partner, discuss the questions. Refer to the outline in exercise **A**.

1. What topics did the introduction cover?
2. Which items are main ideas? Which items are details?

🎧 **C** | **Listening for Main Ideas.** Listen to the entire lecture and answer the questions.

1. Check (✔) each effect of the explosion that the speaker mentions.
  ____ a. People were forced to leave their homes.
  ____ b. Animals died from exposure to radiation.
  ____ c. Young people became ill with thyroid cancer.
  ____ d. Billions of dollars were spent on health and cleanup costs.
  ____ e. Modern nuclear power plants are built with containment structures.
2. What happened to the town of Pripyat?
  a. It was abandoned.
  b. It burned to the ground.
  c. It was turned into a tourist attraction.
3. What is surprising about Chernobyl today?
  a. The residents of Pripyat have returned.
  b. Many animals have come back to the area.
  c. The radiation from the explosion has disappeared.

🎧 **D** | **Outlining.** Listen again. Continue the outline from exercise **A** on page 66. Complete the outline with details from the lecture. (*See page 206 of the Independent Student Handbook for more information on outlining.*)

C. The Chernobyl plant today
  1. Still extremely _____
  2. There are plans to build a _____
D. Radioactivity
  1. Many areas still contaminated with cesium _____
  2. Half-life of _____ years
E. The exclusion zone today
  1. _____ people live there
  2. Animals have returned, for ex., _____

### After Listening

👥 **Discussion.** With a partner, answer the questions. Use your notes as well as your own ideas.

1. Describe the town of Pripyat before and after the disaster.
2. These days, a small number of tourists travel to Chernobyl. Would you go there if you had the opportunity?

## Language Function

### Emphasizing Important Information

Here are some expressions used to emphasize important information.

*Don't forget that . . .*
*Let me stress that . . .*
*I want to emphasize that . . .*
*I would like to stress that . . .*

*I would like to point out that . . .*
*You need to remember that . . .*
*It is important to note/remember that . . .*

**A** | In the lecture about Chernobyl, the speaker used a number of useful expressions to emphasize her point. Listen to the excerpts and fill in the missing expressions.

1. _____ Chernobyl had no containment structure. This building would have limited the fire and contained the radioactivity.
2. Thyroid cancer can be cured, but _____ survivors must spend a lifetime taking medication.
3. _____, however, that it will be decades before large numbers of people are allowed to come back and live in the exclusion zone.

Wild horses, called Przewalski horses, walk through the Chernobyl exclusion zone. These horses are extinct in the wild and can only be found in a few nature reserves and in the Chernobyl exclusion zone.

**B** | Form a group with two other students. Choose one of the types of energy below and read the facts. Then tell the members of your group what you know about your energy source. Add your own ideas. Emphasize the fact that you think is the most interesting.

> Oil prices are rising. For example, it cost me almost $60 to put gas in my car yesterday. Last year, it would have cost me only $40. Still, it is important to remember that . . .

**Oil**
- The price of oil is rising.
- Oil spills pollute the environment.
- The top three oil-producing countries in the world are Saudi Arabia, Russia, and the United States.

**Coal**
- Coal deposits in the United States contain more energy than all the world's oil reserves combined.
- Coal is a relatively inexpensive energy source.
- Coal mining is dangerous. Between 1969 and 2000, more than 20,000 coal miners were killed.

**Wind**
- Wind power is clean, but is sometimes very noisy.
- The world will never run out of wind.
- Denmark gets 20 percent of its electricity from wind power.

The **"Exploring Spoken English"** section allows students to examine and practice specific grammar points and language functions from the unit while enabling them to sharpen their listening and speaking skills.

Lesson A closes with a **full page of "Speaking" activities** including pair and group work activities, increasing learner confidence when communicating in English.

**A variety of activity types** simulate the academic classroom, where multiple skills must be applied simultaneously for success.

## SPEAKING

### Role-Playing a Town Meeting

**A** | Form a group with three other students. You will role-play a city council meeting about building a nuclear power plant. Read the situation and the role cards. Assign two students to each role.

**Situation:** The city council has approved a plan to build a nuclear power plant in your city. A small group of residents are against the plan. They are going to meet with city council members to discuss their concerns.

**Role #1: Residents against the Nuclear Power Plant**

1. Nuclear power plants aren't safe. We don't want a nuclear accident to happen here.
2. Nuclear power plants produce waste that is dangerous for many years.
3. People who live near a nuclear power plant might get cancer.

**Role #2: City Council Members**

1. Nuclear safety technology has greatly advanced in recent years.
2. France, Belgium, and Slovakia rely on nuclear power for more than 50 percent of their electricity. There have been no big nuclear accidents in those countries.
3. Nuclear power could help us stop using oil.

**B** | Work with the group member who shares your role. Think of more arguments to support your point. In addition, try to think of responses to the other side's arguments.

> I think they will say that . . .

> If they say that, we should emphasize that . . .

**C** | **Role-Playing.** Role-play the discussion in your group. Use expressions of emphasis when appropriate.

> Thank you for meeting with us. We have a few concerns about this nuclear power plant.

> I understand. First of all, let me stress that we will do everything possible to make this power plant safe.

### Student to Student: Conceding a Point

In a debate or discussion, people often argue from different points of view. If an argument is very convincing to you, you can let the other person know that you agree with their point or that you accept that their point is true. Here are some expressions to concede a point.

*Good point.*
*Fair enough.*
*I'll give you that.*

The **"Viewing" section** works as a content-bridge between Lesson A and Lesson B and includes two pages of activities based on a fascinating video from National Geographic.

Solar cells turn sunlight into electricity.

# SOLAR POWER

## Before Viewing

**Understanding Visuals.** Read the information. Use the words in blue to label the diagram.

There are many different kinds of solar power systems. This diagram shows how parabolic trough solar power works.

1. Sunlight hits curved mirrors that direct all the light and heat to the middle of the mirror.
2. In the middle of the mirror, a tube filled with synthetic¹ oil is heated to about 700°F.
3. The oil runs into a boiler where it turns water into steam.
4. The steam spins an electric turbine, which turns and makes electricity.

¹**Synthetic** products are made from chemicals or artificial substances rather than from natural sources.

## While Viewing

**A** | Watch the video. Fill in the blanks with the word or words you hear.

The most powerful source of (1) _____ on the planet is actually out in space. It's (2) _____. More energy falls as sunlight on the United States in a single day than it uses in a (3) _____. But it's been difficult to turn that sunlight into (4) _____. Many people already use some (5) _____. But the world's need for power is great, and for solar power to be an alternative to other energy sources, it has to be both affordable and (6) _____.

**B** | Watch the video again. Check (✔) the five true statements.

1. _____ Sacramento doesn't use much solar power.
2. _____ Many new homes have solar cells.
3. _____ Many people drive solar-powered cars.
4. _____ Solar panels shade parking lots.
5. _____ Solar panels shade city buildings.
6. _____ Sacramento gets lower prices by buying a lot of solar panels at one time.
7. _____ Solar power is very expensive to residents of Sacramento.
8. _____ People can sell electricity back to the power company.

**C** | **Viewing for Specific Information.** Watch the video again. Circle the best answer to each question.

1. Where is the Kramer Solar Junction facility located?
   a. In the mountains
   b. In a desert
   c. By the sea
2. How many people can the facility provide power for?
   a. Half a million
   b. Five million
   c. Eight and a half million
3. What happens on days when there is no sun?
   a. The facility buys back power from customers.
   b. The facility uses power from batteries.
   c. The facility uses backup natural gas generators.
4. What does the facility produce a lot of?
   a. Power
   b. Carbon dioxide
   c. Smog

Ladybug robots crawl down a leaf. The robots are powered by solar power collectors attached to their backs.

## After Viewing

**Critical Thinking.** With a partner, discuss the questions.

1. What are some problems that could occur when using solar power?
2. In general, do you think the government should be responsible for developing alternative energies? Or, should it be left to private corporations to develop alternative energies? Explain your answer.
3. Mirrors now cover 1000 acres of the Mojave Desert at the Kramer Solar Junction power facility. What impact could this have on the local environment there?

● **A DVD for each level** contains 10 authentic videos from National Geographic specially adapted for English language learners.

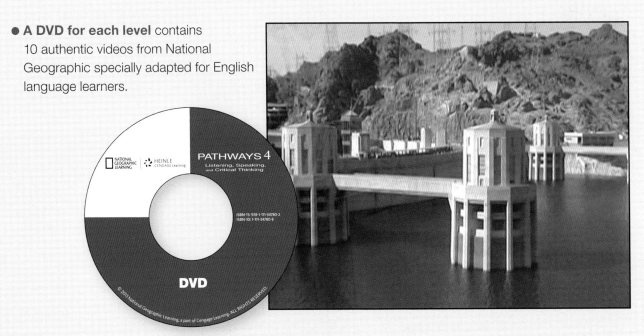

NATIONAL GEOGRAPHIC LEARNING · HEINLE CENGAGE Learning

PATHWAYS 4
Listening, Speaking, and Critical Thinking

ISBN-13: 978-1-111-34780-2
ISBN-10: 1-111-34780-8

**DVD**

©2013 National Geographic Learning, a part of Cengage Learning. ALL RIGHTS RESERVED.

**Critical thinking activities** are integrated in every unit, encouraging continuous engagement in developing academic skills.

An **"Engage" section** at the end of the unit challenges learners with an end-of-unit presentation project. Speaking tips are offered for formal and informal group communication, instructing students to interact appropriately in different academic situations.

UNIT
4

### ENGAGE: Creating and Using Visuals in a Presentation

Your group is going to deliver a presentation to the class about an unusual source of energy. To support your presentation, your group will make a poster or a slide presentation with pictures, graphs, or other visual information. Your visual should include answers to these questions:

1. What is an unusual source of energy?
2. How does this energy source work?
3. What are the advantages and disadvantages of using this energy source?

**A | Discussion.** Form a group of two or three students. Examine the list of unusual energy sources and select one to research.

This biomass plant burns rice to generate electricity.

biodiesel          hydrogen fuel cells
biomass            methane from landfills
energy-generating floors    sugar
ethanol            tidal or ocean power

**B | Researching.** Outside of class, research your topic online or in the library. Use the outline below as a guide while you take notes about your topic. Find several images that relate to your energy source. (See page 212 of the Independent Student Handbook for more information on doing research.)

I. Type of energy
   A. Description
   B. Source
II. Examples of how the energy is used
   A. Places
   B. Purposes
III. Advantages
IV. Disadvantages
V. Future of this form of energy

**C | Planning a Presentation.** As a group, use your notes from exercise **B** and your images to create a poster or slide presentation about your energy source. Be sure that your poster or slide presentation answers the three questions in the box at the top of the page.

**D | Presentation.** When you give your presentation, all group members should speak. Be sure to explain the images you present, and answer any questions from your audience.

**Presentation Skills: Fighting Nervousness**

It is normal to be a little nervous at the beginning of a presentation. However, the first impression you make on your audience is very important. Make an effort to speak slowly and calmly at the beginning of your presentation. Memorizing the first few sentences you plan to say can sometimes help. Soon you will begin to feel more comfortable and gain confidence.

80 | UNIT 4

**"Presentation Skills" boxes** offer helpful tips and suggestions for successful academic presentations.

A 19-page **"Independent Student Handbook"** is conveniently located in the back of the book and provides helpful self-study strategies for students to become better independent learners.

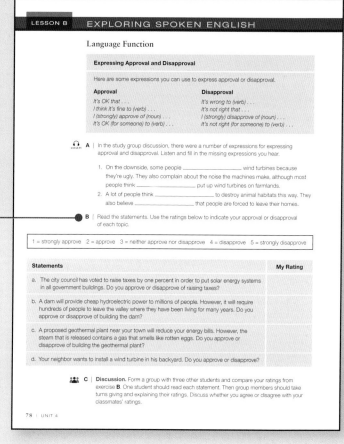

### Language Function

**Expressing Approval and Disapproval**

Here are some expressions you can use to express approval or disapproval.

| Approval | Disapproval |
|---|---|
| It's OK that . . . | It's wrong to (verb) . . . |
| I think it's fine to (verb) . . . | It's not right that . . . |
| I (strongly) approve of (noun) . . . | I (strongly) disapprove of (noun) . . . |
| It's OK (for someone) to (verb) . . . | It's not right (for someone) to (verb) . . . |

**A |** In the study group discussion, there were a number of expressions for expressing approval and disapproval. Listen and fill in the missing expressions you hear.

1. On the downside, some people _____ wind turbines because they're ugly. They also complain about the noise the machines make, although most people think _____ put up wind turbines on farmlands.

2. A lot of people think _____ to destroy animal habitats this way. They also believe _____ that people are forced to leave their homes.

**B |** Read the statements. Use the ratings below to indicate your approval or disapproval of each topic.

1 = strongly approve   2 = approve   3 = neither approve nor disapprove   4 = disapprove   5 = strongly disapprove

| Statements | My Rating |
|---|---|
| a. The city council has voted to raise taxes by one percent in order to put solar energy systems in all government buildings. Do you approve or disapprove of raising taxes? | |
| b. A dam will provide cheap hydroelectric power to millions of people. However, it will require hundreds of people to leave the valley where they have been living for many years. Do you approve or disapprove of building the dam? | |
| c. A proposed geothermal plant near your town will reduce your energy bills. However, the steam that is released contains a gas that smells like rotten eggs. Do you approve or disapprove of building the geothermal plant? | |
| d. Your neighbor wants to install a wind turbine in his backyard. Do you approve or disapprove? | |

**C | Discussion.** Form a group with three other students and compare your ratings from exercise **B**. One student should read each statement. Then group members should take turns giving and explaining their ratings. Discuss whether you agree or disagree with your classmates' ratings.

78 | UNIT 4

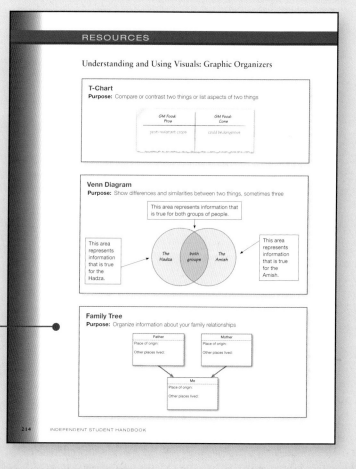

### RESOURCES

**Understanding and Using Visuals: Graphic Organizers**

**T-Chart**
**Purpose:** Compare or contrast two things or list aspects of two things

| GM Food: Pros | GM Food: Cons |
|---|---|
| pest-resistant crops | could be dangerous |

**Venn Diagram**
**Purpose:** Show differences and similarities between two things, sometimes three

This area represents information that is true for both groups of people.

This area represents information that is true for the Hadza.

The Hadza | both groups | The Amish

This area represents information that is true for the Amish.

**Family Tree**
**Purpose:** Organize information about your family relationships

| Father | Mother |
|---|---|
| Place of origin: | Place of origin: |
| Other places lived: | Other places lived: |

Me
Place of origin:
Other places lived:

214   INDEPENDENT STUDENT HANDBOOK

## For the Teacher:

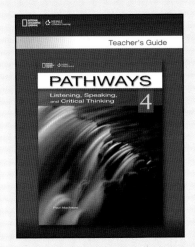

A **Teacher's Guide** is available in an easy-to-use format and includes teacher's notes, expansion activities, and answer keys for activities in the student book.

Perfect for integrating language practice with exciting visuals, **video clips from National Geographic** bring the sights and sounds of our world into the classroom.

**The Assessment CD-ROM with Exam*View*®** is a test-generating software program with a data bank of ready-made questions designed to allow teachers to assess students quickly and effectively.

Bringing a new dimension to the language learning classroom, the **Classroom Presentation Tool CD-ROM** makes instruction clearer and learning easier through interactive activities, audio and video clips, and Presentation Worksheets.

## For the Student:

The **Student Book** helps students achieve academic success in and outside of the classroom.

**Audio CDs** contain the audio recordings for the exercises in the student books.

MyELT. Powered by MyELT, the **Online Workbook** has both teacher-led and self-study options. It contains 10 National Geographic video clips, supported by interactive, automatically graded activities that practice the skills learned in the student books.

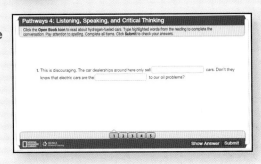

Visit elt.heinle.com/pathways for additional teacher and student resources.

# LISTENING AND TEXT

**5-7,10:** Adapted from "Vanishing Venice," by Cathy Newman: National Geographic Magazine, August 2009, **14-16:** Adapted from, "The Singapore Solution," by Mark Jacobson: National Geographic Magazine, January 2010, **19:** Adapted from "Urban Fishing Catches on in Rebounding Rivers" by James Owen: National Geographic Daily News, May 17, 2010, **25:** Adapted from "Forests of the Tide," by Kennedy Warne: National Geographic Magazine, February 2007, **26-27:** Adapted from "Last One," by Verlyn Klinkenborg: National Geographic Magazine, January 2009,

**34:** Adapted from "Freshwater Hero," National Geographic Web site, **35:** Adapted from "Wolf Wars" by Douglas Chadwick: National Geographic Magazine, March 2010, **36-37:** Adapted from "Hunters: For the Love of the Land," by Robert M. Poole: National Geographic Magazine, November 2007, **46-47:** Adapted from "The Enigma of Beauty," by Cathy Newman, National Geographic Magazine, January 2000, **46-47:** Adapted from "New 'Golden' Ratios for Facial Beauty," by Pamela Pallett et al., National Institute of Health, January 25, 2010, **56-57:** Adapted from "Dreamweavers," by Cathy Newman: National Geographic Web site, January 1, 2003. **56-57:** Adapted from "Artificial Spider Silk Could

Be Used for Armor, More," by Brian Handwerk: National Geographic Daily News, January 14, 2005, **64:** Adapted from "Is Another Deepwater Disaster Inevitable?," by Joel K. Bourne, Jr.: National Geographic Magazine, October 2010, **66-67:** Adapted from "The Long Shadow of Chernobyl," by Richard Stone: National Geographic Magazine, April 2006, **84-87:** Adapted from "Human Journey" by James Shreeve: National Geographic Magazine, March 2006, **84-87:** Adapted from "From Africa to Astoria by Way of Everywhere," by James Shreeve: National Geographic Web site, August 17, 2009, **96-97:** Adapted from "Heartbreak on the Serengeti" by Robert M. Poole: National Geographic Magazine, February 2006.

# PHOTOS

**1:** Richard Levine/Alamy, **3:** Jodi Cobb/National Geographic Image Collection, **3:** Fritz Hoffmann/National Geographic Image Collection, **4:** Atelier Tekuto, **4:** Andy Z/Used under license from Shutterstock.com, **4:** Frances Roberts/Alamy, **5:** Jo Chambers/Shutterstock.com, **6:** Jodi Cobb/National Geographic Image Collection, **9:** Caitlin Mirra/Shutterstock.com, **11:** Mike Theiss/National Geographic Image Collection, **12:** Frans Lemmens/SuperStock, **13:** Matt Fletcher/Lonely Planet Images/Alamy, **13:** Rich Carey/Shutterstock.com, **14:** Caro/Alamy, **14:** Toshifumi Kitamura/AFP/Getty Images, **16:** Joseph Calev/Shutterstock.com, **19:** James Owen, **21:** Brian J. Skerry/National Geographic Image Collection, **22:** Pi-Lens/Shutterstock.com, **22:** Jason Lugo/iStockphoto.com, **22-23:** Beverly Joubert/National Geographic Image Collection, **24:** All Canada Photos/SuperStock, **25:** Tim Laman/National Geographic Image Collection, **26:** John A. Anderson/Shutterstock.com, **26:** Joel Sartore/National Geographic Image Collection, **28:** Gary Meszaros/Photo Researchers, Inc., **29:** Alexandr Pakhnyushchyy/iStockphoto.com, **29:** CraigRJD/iStockphoto.com, **32:** BsChan/Shutterstock, **33:** Null/FLPA/Alamy, **34:** Joel Sartore/National Geographic Image Collection, **35:** Len Tillim/iStockphoto.com, **36:** Bruno Barbey, Magnum/National Geographic Image Collection, **40:** Perrush/

Shutterstock.com, **41:** George Steinmetz/National Geographic Image Collection, **42:** GoGo Images/Jupiter Images, **42:** Greg Dale/National Geographic Image Collection, **42-43:** Mike Theiss/National Geographic Image Collection, **44:** Justin Guariglia/National Geographic Image Collection, **45:** esolla/iStockphoto, **46:** Reprinted from Vision Research, Vol 50, No 2, 25th January 2010, Pallett et al, "New 'Golden' ratios for facial beauty" with permission from Elsevier, **47:** Peter Zagar/National Geographic Image Collection, **49:** Demid Borodin/Shutterstock, **50:** Todd Gipstein/National Geographic Image Collection, **52:** Sarah Leen/National Geographic Image Collection, **52:** Joe McNally/National Geographic Image Collection, **53:** photobywayne/Alamy, **53:** Sarah Leen/National Geographic Image Collection, **54:** John Macdougall/AFP/Getty Images, **55:** Cary Wolinsky/National Geographic Image Collection, **56:** Designer: Alex Soza/Photographer: Peter Svendsen, **56:** Tom Vickers/Splash/Newscom, **56:** Yoshikazu Tsuno/AFP/Getty Images, **58:** Natali Glado/Shutterstock.com, **60:** AJ Wilhelm/National Geographic Image Collection, **60:** Mike Theiss/National Geographic Image Collection, **61:** Hervé Lenain/Hemis/Corbis, **62-63:** Joel Sartore/National Geographic Image Collection, **63:** James M Phelps, Jr/Shutterstock.com, **63:** Michael Utech/Vetta Collection/iStockphoto, **64:** Tyrone Turner/National Geographic Image Collection,

**65:** Brendan Howard/Shutterstock.com, **68:** Gerd Ludwig/National Geographic Image Collection, **69:** huyangshu/Shutterstock.com, **69:** nito/Shutterstock.com, **69:** oorka, 2009/Used under license from Shutterstock.com, **72:** Tobias Machhaus/Shutterstock.com, **73:** George Steinmetz/National Geographic Image Collection, **74:** Samuel Acosta/Shutterstock.com, **74:** Image copyright Belinda Pretorius, 2010 Used under license from Shutterstock.com, **75:** Annie Griffiths/National Geographic Image Collection, **79:** Angela Hampton/Angela Hampton Picture Library/Alamy, **80:** Sarah Leen/National Geographic Image Collection, **81:** Norbert Rosing/National Geographic Image Collection, **82:** Bill Bachman/Alamy, **83:** Joe Mcnally/National Geographic Image Collection, **84:** Jim Richardson/National Geographic Image Collection, **86:** Anthony Peritore, **86:** Piero Gherardi, **86:** Valerie Chazottes Louvat, **86:** Lisa Hopgood, **89:** image copyright Paul Banton/used under license from www.shutterstock.com, **89:** mmm/Shutterstock.com, **92:** Beverly Joubert/National Geographic Image Collection, **93:** Ralph Lee Hopkins/National Geographic Image Collection, **94:** Roy Toft/National Geographic Image Collection Stock, **95:** Iv Mirin/Shutterstock.com, **96:** Randy Olson/National Geographic Image Collection, **96:** Randy Olson/National Geographic Image Collection, **99:** Joe McNally/National Geographic Image Collection

# MAP AND ILLUSTRATION

**2-3:** National Geographic Maps; **6:** National Geographic Maps; **7:** www.cartoonstock.com; **10:** Fernando Baptista and Alejandro Tumas,

NGM staff; **12:** National Geographic Maps; **16:** National Geographic Maps; **32:** National Geographic Maps; **64:** National Geographic Maps; **66:** National Geographic Maps; **82-83:** NGM Maps/National Geographic

Image Collection; **85:** Gregory Manchess/National Geographic Image Collection; **92:** National Geographic Maps; **92:** Map courtesy of Roy Safaris–Tanzania

# Urban Challenges

ACADEMIC PATHWAYS

## Think and Discuss

1. What are some of the problems that modern cities face? How can cities solve these problems?

2. Would you move to a city that is dealing with challenges such as overcrowding? Explain.

In New York City, people walk by a mural by a Brazilian graffiti artist.

NORTH
AMERICA

EUROPE

Reykjavík          •Tórshavn

Copenhagen
Amsterdam
Dublin
London
Brussels
Paris
Luxembourg
Monaco
Andorra
Barcelona
Madrid
Lisbon                Algiers
Gibraltar
Casablanca

Laayoune

Toronto
Chicago              New York
                     Philadelphia
Los Angeles

St.-Pierre

•Hamilton

Miami
Nassau
Havana          Cockburn Town
Santa Domingo    San Juan
Port-au-Prince   Charlotte Amalie
Mexico City   George Town•   Road Town
              Kingston     •St. John's
Belize City   Basse-Terre  •Pointe-à-Pitre
Guatemala City            Roseau   Fort-de-France
San Salvador             Kingstown  Castries
Tegucigalpa   Oranjestad•         Bridgetown
Managua       Willemstad   •St. George's
San José      Panama City  Port of Spain
              Caracas
Bogotá                    Georgetown
                          Paramaribo
                          •Cayenne

Nouakchott

Praia•
Dakar
Banjul        Bamako
Bissau        Ouagad
Conakry
Freetown                Accra
Monrovia
Abidjan      Lomé
São Te

Guayaquil

SOUTH
AMERICA

Lima

La Paz

Belo Horizonte

São Paulo    Rio de Janeiro
Asunción

Papeete•

**Urban agglomerations, 2007**

Largest        Other
city in        cities above
country        5 million

Tokyo    Urban agglomeration with more
         than 10 million people (megacity)

Chicago  Urban agglomeration with more
         than 5 million people

La Paz   Largest urban agglomeration
         per country or possession

Santiago

Buenos Aires    •Montevideo

•Stanley

## Bigger Cities, New Challenges

Cars fill the streets of Bangkok, Thailand. As cities get larger, new challenges such as traffic jams become important issues.

## More People, Less Space

Crowds fill a railroad station in Guangdong, China. As the world's population grows, competition for space is a challenge in many large cities.

ASIA

Helsinki
Tallinn
Riga
Minsk
Vilnius
Warsaw
Vienna
Bratislava
Budapest
Zagreb
Belgrade
Bucharest
pje
Sofia
Athens
Nicosia
Tel Aviv-Yafo
Cairo
Gaza City

Moscow
Kiev
Chişinău

Istanbul
Yerevan
Ḥalab
(Aleppo)
Beirut
Amman
Baghdad

Tbilisi
Baku
Tashkent
Ashgabat
Dushanbe
Kabul
Tehran
Kuwait City
Manama
Dubai
Muscat

Bishkek
Almaty

Lahore
Delhi
Kathmandu
Phuntsholing
Kolkata
(Calcutta)
Dhaka

Ulaanbaatar

Pyongyang
Beijing
Seoul
Tianjin
Wuhan
Chongqing
Shanghai
Osaka
Tokyo

Shenzhen
Guangzhou
Hong Kong

RICA
Khartoum
N'Djamena

Riyadh
Doha

Karachi
Ahmadabad
Pune
Mumbai
(Bombay)
Hyderabad
Bangalore
(Bengaluru)
Chennai
(Madras)
Colombo
Male

Yangon
(Rangoon)
Bangkok
Phnom Penh
Ho Chi Minh City
Vientiane

Manila

Capital Hill
Hagåtña (Agana)

Asmara
Sanaa
Djibouti
Addis Ababa

Chittagong

Melekeok
Palikir

Bangui
Kampala
Kigali
Bujumbura
Nairobi
Mogadishu

Bandar Seri Begawan
Kuala Lumpur
Singapore

Na

Dar es Salaam
Victoria
Jakarta

Dili

Port Moresby
Honiara

Moroni
Lilongwe
Lusaka
Harare
Antananarivo
St.-Denis
Port Louis

Port Vila

Gaborone
Johannesburg
Maseru
Maputo
Mbabane

AUSTRALIA

Nouméa

Sydney

Auckland

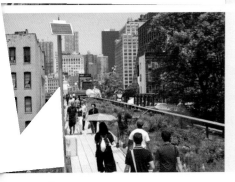

track 1-2 **A** | **Meaning from Context.** Read and listen to the information about the ways that some cities are meeting new challenges. Notice the words in blue. These are words you will hear and use in Lesson A.

Finding affordable land for housing is a **challenge** in many of the world's largest cities. Some **residents** of Tokyo, Japan, have found a solution to this problem. They are building homes on pieces of land as small as 344 square feet (32 square meters). These "micro-homes" allow people to live close to central Tokyo and cost much less than other homes in the city. Many micro-homes have several floors and big windows that **maximize** sunlight.

Many cities have problems with air pollution and smog[1]. What can big cities do to **regulate** the amount of air pollution and smog **generated** by cars and factories? An Italian company has come up with an **innovative** tool to reduce pollution: smog-eating cement. The cement contains a substance that **converts** pollution into harmless chemicals. The harmless chemicals wash off roadways when it rains. Smog-eating materials are also being used in roof tiles in Los Angeles, California, the smoggiest city in the United States.

Cities must find creative ways to build public parks, gardens, and outdoor areas when space is limited. In New York City, the High Line was an unattractive black steel **structure** that once supported railroad tracks. Today, the High Line has been **restored** as an elevated urban park. The park was **financed** by donations, and now it is one of the most inviting public spaces in the city. Visitors can walk through the gardens, relax on the sundeck, and attend public art exhibits and special events.

[1]**Smog** is a combination of smoke and fog that can damage the health of humans, plants, and animals.

**B** | Match each sentence beginning to its ending to complete each definition. Use context clues from exercise **A** to understand the words in blue. Use your dictionary to help you.

1. The **residents** of a house or area are ____
2. To **finance** something means ____
3. If you **maximize** something, ____
4. A **challenge** is ____
5. An **innovation** is ____
6. If you **restore** an old painting, ____
7. To **regulate** something means ____
8. When you **generate** something, ____
9. A **structure** is ____
10. To **convert** one thing into another means ____

a. you repair and clean it.
b. to change it so that it can be used for another purpose.
c. the people who live there.
d. you produce it, or cause it to be produced.
e. something new and creative.
f. you increase it as much as possible.
g. something that has been built.
h. a difficult job that requires effort.
i. to control the way it is done.
j. to pay for it.

**A | Using a Dictionary.** Complete the chart with the correct form of each word. An X indicates that the word form does not exist. Use your dictionary to help you. *(See page 209 of the Independent Student Handbook for more information on using a dictionary.)*

|     | Noun | Verb | Adjective |
| --- | --- | --- | --- |
| 1. | challenge | *challenge* | |
| 2. | | convert | X |
| 3. | | finance | |
| 4. | | generate | X |
| 5. | | | innovative |
| 6. | | maximize | |
| 7. | | regulate | |
| 8. | resident | | |
| 9. | | restore | |
| 10. | structure | | |

**B | Read a tour guide's explanation of an unusual challenge facing the city of Venice, Italy. Fill in each blank with the correct form of a word from exercise A above.**

Welcome to Venice, everybody! To start our tour today, I want to tell you about a (1) _____ we face in our beautiful city: floods. You see, a large portion of Venice was built on a salt marsh.[1] City planners had to find a way to (2) _____ space and use every part of the marsh. Builders placed hundreds of wooden logs deep into the marsh. Then they placed building foundations[2] on top of the logs. By doing this, they were able to (3) _____ the salt marsh into land for farming. But the salt marsh is like a giant sponge. The weight of the city pushes down on the salt marsh and buildings slowly sink into the water. High tides, called *acqua alta*, are also a problem. Now, Venice floods on a regular basis. Venetian (4) _____ are used to the floods, but our old and beautiful buildings suffer. Many (5) _____ are damaged by the water and the (6) _____ of these buildings is very expensive.

The city is now building water barriers that will stop seawater from flooding the city. This (7) _____ project is called MOSE, and it will be completed soon. The cost of this project is already more than seven billion dollars. Some people argue that the project violates government (8) _____ and is illegal. Others believe that the water barriers will interfere with the beauty of the city and will cause tourists to leave. Let's hope this does not happen, because tourism (9) _____ business for shops, restaurants, and hotels. (10) _____ support is necessary to help pay for the MOSE project. So thank you for coming to Venice!

[1] A **salt marsh** is an area of flat, wet ground that is sometimes covered by salt water.
[2] A **foundation** is a layer of bricks or concrete that a structure is built on.

# Before Listening

Thousands of tourists fill the streets of Venice.

👥 **Predicting Content.** Look at the photo of tourists in Venice. Can you guess how many tourists visit Venice each year? How do tourists help the city? How do they hurt it? Discuss your ideas with a partner. (*See page 202 of the Independent Student Handbook for more information on predicting.*)

# Listening: A Lecture

| Critical Thinking Focus: Identifying the Lecture Topic |
| --- |
| Lecture introductions often have two parts. In the first part, the speaker provides background information about the topic, or reviews what was covered in earlier lectures. In the second part of the introduction, the speaker announces the specific topic they plan to discuss and explains how they will present the information. Correctly identifying the lecture topic can help you organize your lecture notes. |

🎧 track 1-3 **A** | Listen to the lecture introduction. Which *specific* topic is this lecture about? Circle the correct answer.

1. The problem of flooding
2. The MOSE project
3. Problems caused by tourists

🎧 track 1-4 **B** | **Listening for Main Ideas.** Listen to the lecture and complete the main ideas about the problems and benefits of tourism. (*See page 203 of the Independent Student Handbook for more information on listening for main ideas.*)

| Problems of Tourism | Benefits of Tourism |
| --- | --- |
| 1. City services _____ | 1. Generates _____ |
| 2. Higher prices for _____ | 2. Money helps city _____ |
| 3. Higher _____ in tourist areas | 3. Many Venetians have jobs related to _____ |
| 4. Bad _____ problem | |
| 5. The city's population is _____ | |

👥 **C** | With a partner, compare your answers from exercise **B**. Did you both list the same main ideas?

**D** | **Listening for Details.** Listen again and answer the questions about details in the lecture.

1. How many tourists visited Venice in one holiday weekend?
   a. 60,000
   b. 80,000
   c. 21 million
2. What is NOT found in the Rialto Market area?
   a. Grocery stores
   b. Souvenir shops
   c. A beach
3. What did a 1999 law make it easier to do?
   a. Convert residences to hotels or guest houses
   b. Increase the cost of garbage collection
   c. Create affordable housing for young people
4. What is the population of Venice today?
   a. Around 120,000
   b. Around 80,000
   c. Around 60,000
5. What did the speaker say about the unemployment rate in Venice?
   a. It is higher than in the rest of Italy.
   b. It is lower than in the rest of Italy.
   c. It is lower in the summer than in other seasons.

## After Listening

**A** | **Making Inferences.** Discuss these questions with a partner.

1. Based on the lecture, what is the attitude of Venetian residents toward tourists? Use information from the listening to support your answer.
2. What is the lecturer's attitude about Venice's future?
3. Look at the cartoon. Do you think it is funny? Discuss the ways in which it relates to the lecture you just heard.

**B** | Form a group with two or three other students. Look at the cartoon. As a group, create a caption for the cartoon. Share your caption with the class.

# Language Function

> **Introducing a Topic**
>
> During a presentation or a formal conversation, we often use special phrases and expressions to introduce a topic. These expressions help listeners to identify main ideas and follow along with a presentation or conversation. Here are some common phrases to introduce a new topic.
>
> | | |
> |---|---|
> | *To begin with . . .* | *Let me add that . . .* |
> | *I'd like to focus on . . .* | *Another point I want to make is . . .* |
> | *Today's topic is . . .* | *Today, we're going to cover . . .* |
> | *Let's move on to . . .* | *What I want to do today is . . .* |

**A** | In the lecture, the speaker used a number of expressions for introducing a topic. Listen to the sentences and fill in the expressions.

track 1-5

1. OK, everyone, _____ continue our discussion about cities and the challenges they face . . .

2. So, _____, let's review a few of the points we've discussed so far.

3. _____ there is a serious housing problem in Venice.

4. _____ that many people in Venice have jobs related to tourism.

**B** | Reread the expressions for introducing a topic. Which expressions are for introducing topics at the beginning of a talk? Which expressions are for introducing topics later on in a talk? Write each expression in the correct column.

| Introducing a Topic at the Beginning of a Talk | Introducing a Topic Later on in a Talk |
|---|---|
| | |

**C** | You have learned about two of Venice's challenges. Imagine that you are explaining one of the challenges to a new student. Choose one of the roles below and explain the problem to a partner. Use expressions for introducing a topic in your discussion.

> **Student A:** Flooding in Venice (Refer to exercise **B**, page 5.)
>
> **Student B:** Tourism in Venice (Refer to pages 6–7 and CD 1, Track 4.)

# Grammar

## The Passive Voice

We use the active voice to emphasize the agent, or the "doer," of an action:

*During the* acqua alta, ***people wear boots*** *instead of shoes.*

We use the passive voice when the agent of a sentence is not known or is not important. Instead, the passive voice emphasizes the object of the action.

*During the* acqua alta, ***boots are worn*** *instead of shoes.*

The passive voice consists of a form of *be* + the past participle of the verb.

| Verb Tense | Passive Voice |
|---|---|
| Simple present | *During the Carnival celebration, masks* ***are worn****.* |
| Simple past | *The walkways* ***weren't set up*** *today.* |
| Future | *The barriers* ***will be (are going to be) constructed****.* |
| Present continuous | *Flood barriers* ***are being constructed****.* |
| Present perfect | *Their house* ***hasn't been sold****.* |
| Modal, simple present | *The house* ***can't be converted*** *into a hotel.* |

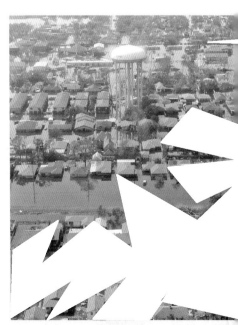

Hurricane Katrina flooded the city of New Orleans, Louisiana.

**A** | Complete each sentence with the passive voice of the verb in parentheses. Use the correct verb tense.

1. New Orleans _____ badly _____ (damage) during Hurricane Katrina in 2005.
2. Eighty percent of the city _____ (flood).
3. Some parts of New Orleans _____ still _____ (rebuild).
4. There have been many meetings to discuss how a similar disaster _____ (can, avoid) in the future.
5. A conference on this subject _____ (hold) next year.
6. Meanwhile, tourists are returning to New Orleans, and many conventions _____ (hold) there every year.

👥 **B** | Study the diagram of the MOSE flood barrier project in Venice. Work with a partner to complete the conversation about the diagram. Complete the sentences with the active or passive voice of the verb in parentheses. Use the correct tense.

How It Works:
1. Hollow steel gates filled with water lie in areas built into the Venice lagoon floor.
2. When a flood is predicted, air is pumped into the gates. This makes the gates float and allows them to rise within a half hour.
3. Fully elevated, the gates separate the sea from the lagoon. When the flood stops, water flows back into the gates to cover them.

1. **A:** Where _will_ the barriers _be constructed_ (construct)?

   **B:** They _____ (construct) in the three places where water enters the Venice lagoon from the Adriatic Sea.

2. **A:** What _____ the barriers _____ (consist) of?

   **B:** They _____ (consist) of 78 giant gates, 92 feet (28 meters) wide and 65 feet (20 meters) across.

3. **A:** What _____ the gates _____ (attach) to?

   **B:** They _____ (attach) to giant concrete bases lying on the sea floor.

4. **A:** When _____ the gates _____ (raise)?

   **B:** Whenever a high tide _____ (predict) and there is a danger of flooding in the city.

5. **A:** How _____ the gates _____ (raise)?

   **B:** Air _____ (pump) into hollow panels in the gate. This _____ (force) the gate to rise and form a barrier against the waves.

6. **A:** When _____ the project _____ (complete)?

   **B:** If everything goes as planned, it _____ (complete) in 2012.

👥 **C** | **Understanding Visuals.** Work with your partner and practice the conversation from exercise **B**. Then discuss the MOSE diagram with your partner. Based on the diagram, do you think the MOSE barrier will stop floods? Explain your opinions.

## Discussing Pros and Cons of Tourism

 **A** | **Critical Thinking.** Form a group with two or three other students. Look at the list of topics below. How does tourism affect each of these areas? Discuss your ideas with your group. Add your own topics to the list.

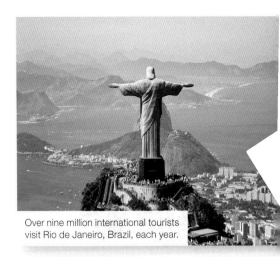

Over nine million international tourists visit Rio de Janeiro, Brazil, each year.

> Public transportation
> Culture (arts, restaurants, and museums)
> Tourist attractions
> Cleanliness
> Job opportunities for residents
> The cost of living
> The city's reputation
> Other: _____

**B** | **Organizing Ideas.** With your group, select a city that you know well. Make notes in the chart about the positive effects (pros) and negative effects (cons) that tourism has on your chosen city.

| City | |
|---|---|
| **Positive Effects (Pros)** | |
| **Negative Effects (Cons)** | |

**C** | **Discussion.** With your group, use your chart from exercise **B** to talk about the effects of tourism on your chosen city. Does tourism have more positive effects or more negative effects?

### Student to Student: Apologizing for Interrupting

Sometimes in pair or group conversations people accidentally interrupt other people. Here are some expressions you can use to apologize for interrupting.

*Sorry.*
*Go ahead.*
*I'm sorry. I didn't mean to cut you off.*
*Sorry. What were you going to say?*
*Oops. Please finish what you were saying.*

# TUAREG FARMERS

Mali
Gossi lake

The Tuareg people were nomads, but today some of them are farmers.

## Before Viewing

**A | Predicting Content.** Lesson A discussed some challenges faced by people in cities. The video you are going to watch is about a problem faced by farmers in Mali. With a partner, look at the map and the photos on pages 12 and 13 and answer the questions.

1. Some Tuareg farmers live next to Lake Gossi. Why do you think they live there?
2. Some elephants stay at Lake Gossi during the dry season. Why do you think they stay there?
3. What problems can you imagine between the farmers and elephants at Lake Gossi? Write three problems you think you might see in the video.

_____

_____

_____

**B | Using a Dictionary.** You will hear these words and phrases in the video. Work with your partner and match each word or phrase with the correct definition. Use your dictionary to help you. =disaster

1. catastrophe (n.)   c
dry Period  2. brush fence (n.)   e
3. drought (n.)   d
4. nightmare (n.)   a
5. nomad (n.)   b

a. a frightening dream; a terrible experience
b. a person who has no permanent home, but moves constantly in search of water and food
c. an unexpected event that causes great suffering
d. an unusually long time during which no rain falls
e. a barrier made from short, strong bushes
small trees/plants

# While Viewing

Lake Gossi in Mali has no rain for many months of the year.

**A** | Look at the problems you listed in exercise **A** in the Before Viewing section. Watch the video. Check the problem(s) the video talks about.

**B** | **Viewing for Main Ideas.** Watch the video again. What do the farmers do to keep elephants out of their gardens? Check (✔) *Yes* for the things you see and *No* for the things you don't see.

| Solutions to the Elephant Problem | Yes | No |
|---|---|---|
| 1. They dig deep holes for the elephants to fall into. | | ✓ |
| 2. They build fences around the gardens to keep the elephants out. | ✓ | |
| 3. They shine lights at the elephants and make a lot of noise. | ✓ | |
| 4. They use guns to shoot at the elephants. | | ✓ |
| 5. They put the elephants in trucks and take them far away. | | ✓ |
| 6. They grow food for the elephants outside of the gardens. | | ✓ |

# After Viewing

**A** | Complete each sentence using the passive voice of the verb in parentheses.

1. The water ___is shared___ (share) between the people and the elephants.
2. Water ___is carried___ (carry) from the lake to the gardens in goatskins.
3. The elephants ___are attracted___ (attract) to the gardens because there is little food available during the dry season.
4. Last night was a nightmare for the farmers. Many crops and trees ___were destroyed___ (destroy).
5. The same struggle ___has been repeated___ (repeat) every year since Omar was a child.

**B** | **Critical Thinking.** Form a group with two or three other students. Look at your answers to exercise **B** in the While Viewing section. There are six ideas in the list, but the farmers don't try all of them. Discuss the other ideas. Why do you think the farmers don't try these ideas?

Elephants need huge amounts of water and food.

**A | Using a Dictionary.** Work with a partner. Match each word with its definition. Use your dictionary to help you.

1. internalize (v.)    _f_
2. conform (v.)    _j_
3. ethnic (adj.)    _a_
4. debatable (adj.)    _h_
5. enforce (v.)    _c_
6. compatible (adj.)    _b_
7. economy (n.)    _i_
8. dominate (v.)    _e_
9. prohibit (v.)    _g_
10. unique (adj.)    _d_

a. relating to a group of people who have the same culture, race, traditions, or background
b. able to exist together
c. to make sure that a rule is obeyed
d. one of a kind
e. to have control of or power over an area
f. to make a belief part of your way of thinking
g. to forbid
h. a topic that can be questioned and is not certain
i. the system by which a country's trade, industry, and money are organized
j. to behave in the same way as most other people

track 1-6 **B |** Read the article and fill in each blank with the correct form of a word from exercise **A**. Then listen and check your answers.

Singapore is one of Asia's most interesting countries. It is surprising that such a small nation has such a powerful (1) _____. Many people believe that Singapore's economic success is because of the leadership of Lee Kuan Yew, Singapore's first Prime Minister. His ideas have (2) _____ the politics of Singapore for decades.

Residents of Singapore

Singapore's model of success is unlike that of any other country. The model is a (3) _____ combination of two ideas: the encouragement of business and the enforcement of strict laws. To follow this model, the people of Singapore have learned to live and work together in an orderly way. There are laws that encourage cooperation between (4) _____ groups, and like all laws in Singapore, they are strictly (5) _____.

Spitting, selling chewing gum, and littering are all (6) _____ by law. While these laws may surprise some visitors, many Singaporeans have (7) _____ them, and for the most part, they follow the rules and laws without thinking about them.

Most Singaporeans believe that strict laws are (8) _____ with an orderly and secure society. They are willing to (9) _____ to rules and laws if it will make life in Singapore more pleasant. Some Singaporeans and some people from other countries, however, may feel that the benefits of these laws are (10) _____.

Lee Kuan Yew

**A | Using a Dictionary.** Complete the chart with the correct form of a word from exercise **A** on page 14. Then complete each sentence with the correct form of the word. Use your dictionary to help you.

| | Noun | Verb | Adjective |
|---|---|---|---|
| 1. | | | debatable |
| 2. | | enforce | |
| 3. | economy | | |
| 4. | | prohibit | |

1. Dogs are _____ on public beaches and in many parks.
2. The two candidates for president are going to hold a public _____.
3. In the United States, a law against chewing gum would not be _____.
4. When my father lost his job, our family was forced to _____.

**B |** Work with a partner. Read the statements about Singapore. Guess if they are true or false. Circle **T** for *true* or **F** for *false*. Then check your answers at the bottom of the page.

1. The cream-colored giant squirrel is a unique animal that lives only in Singapore.　　　　**T**　　**F**
2. The largest ethnic group in Singapore is Malay.　　　　**T**　　**F**
3. In 2010, Singapore's economy had the highest growth rate in the world.　　　　**T**　　**F**
4. In Singapore, eating ice cream in public is prohibited by law.　　　　**T**　　**F**
5. Singapore has a special government agency that enforces anticorruption laws.　　　　**T**　　**F**

**C |** **Self-Reflection.** Form a group with two or three other students. Discuss the following questions.

1. Do you have a goal such as graduating from school that has dominated your actions? In what way has this goal affected you?
2. What is an important value or belief you have internalized?
3. Talk about a time when you chose to conform to what other people were doing. Do you think you made the right choice, or did you regret it later?
4. Are strict laws compatible with your ideas of personal freedom? Explain.

# Before Listening

👥 **Predicting Content.** With a partner, predict the answers to these questions about Singapore.

1. Look at the map. Where is Singapore located? How big do you think it is? How many large cities does it have?
2. Look at the photo at the bottom of the page. Why do you think the Merlion was chosen as the symbol of Singapore? Brainstorm some ideas.

## Listening: A Conversation between Classmates

🎧 track 1-7 **A** | **Listening for Main Ideas.** Read the statements below. Then listen to the conversation about Singapore. Circle **T** for *true* or **F** for *false*.

| | | | |
|---|---|---|---|
| 1. | The word *Singapore* means "lion city." | **T** | **F** |
| 2. | Singapore is rich in natural resources. | **T** | **F** |
| 3. | Nearly all the people of Singapore belong to one ethnic group. | **T** | **F** |
| 4. | Singapore is a small country with a large economy. | **T** | **F** |
| 5. | The spirit of *kiasu* is about enjoying life every minute. | **T** | **F** |
| 6. | Singapore has a strict system of laws. | **T** | **F** |

👥 **B** | Compare your answers to exercise **A** with a partner. Revise the false statements to make them true.

🎧 track 1-7 **C** | **Listening for Details.** Listen again. Fill in the missing information.

1. Singapore started off as a _____ village.
2. Modern Singapore was founded in the year _____.
3. The size of Singapore is about _____ square miles (697 square kilometers).
4. Singapore is _____ percent urbanized.
5. Singapore's economy was ranked the _____ most innovative economy in the world.
6. Lee Kuan Yew's ideas dominated Singapore politics for _____ years.
7. *Kiasu* means "afraid to _____."

## After Listening

👥 **Discussion.** With a partner, discuss the questions.

1. Do you have the spirit of *kiasu*? Explain.
2. In Singapore you can be fined for spitting on the ground and for forgetting to flush a public toilet. Do you think these types of laws would be helpful in your city? Explain.

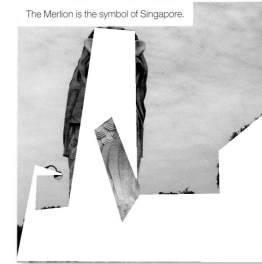

The Merlion is the symbol of Singapore.

# Pronunciation

## Pronouncing the letter *t*

The letter *t* at the end of a word can be pronounced in different ways. Here are three common ways to pronounce *t* at the end of a word:

1. When a word that ends in *t* is followed by a word that begins with a vowel, the *t* is pronounced as a quick *d* sound.
   *that again*          *it is*                *what are*

2. When *t* is followed by a word that begins with a consonant (other than *t* or *d*), hold your teeth and tongue in a *t* position, but do not release any air.
   *not now*             *what really*          *that language*

3. When *t* is followed by a word beginning with the sound /y/, such as *you* or *your*, the *t* is pronounced *ch*.
   *what you*            *that you*             *at your*

**A** | Look at the following word pairs. How is the final *t* of the first word pronounced? Check (✔) your answer.

|  | *d* | no air | *ch* |  |  | *d* | no air | *ch* |
|---|---|---|---|---|---|---|---|---|
| 1. at you | ❏ | ❏ | ❏ | 5. thought your | ❏ | ❏ | ❏ |
| 2. upset about | ❏ | ❏ | ❏ | 6. not yet | ❏ | ❏ | ❏ |
| 3. hit us | ❏ | ❏ | ❏ | 7. eight o'clock | ❏ | ❏ | ❏ |
| 4. what now | ❏ | ❏ | ❏ | 8. not really | ❏ | ❏ | ❏ |

**B** | Listen and check your answers to exercise **A**. Then listen again and repeat the phrases.

**C** | With a partner, practice the following dialogs. Pay attention to the underlined words and be sure to pronounce *t* correctly. When you finish, switch roles and repeat.

1. **A:** I didn't hear what you said.
   **B:** I'm sorry. I'll say it again.

2. **A:** Do you want some coffee?
   **B:** No thanks. But how about some tea?

3. **A:** Is it lunchtime?
   **B:** Not yet.

4. **A:** What are you going to do with those papers?
   **B:** I'm going to put them in the trash.

5. **A:** What are you so upset about?
   **B:** I got a bad grade on that science test.

# Language Function

**Agreeing or Disagreeing**

We use many different expressions to agree or disagree with something that someone has said. Some expressions are mild (gentle). Others are stronger and said with more feeling.

|  | **Agree** |  | **Disagree** |
|---|---|---|---|
| mild | *I agree.* | mild | *I'm not so sure (about that).* |
| ↓ | *I think so too.* | ↓ | *That's debatable.* |
|  | *I think you're right.* |  | *I disagree.* |
|  | *Exactly!* |  | *I don't think so.* |
| strong | *No kidding!* | strong | *No way!* |
|  | *You can say that again!* |  | *That's crazy!* |

**A** | In the conversation about Singapore, the classmates used a number of expressions for agreeing and disagreeing. Listen to the conversation again and write the expressions you hear.

track 1-10

1. **Man:** You know, the Singaporeans I've met all work very hard. They seem to want to be number one in everything.
   **Woman:** _____.

2. **Man:** I think that the laws seem way too strict, don't you?
   **Woman:** Actually, no. _____.

3. **Woman:** In my opinion, I'd rather have strict laws and safe streets than lenient laws and more crime.
   **Man:** Hmmm. _____. I think it's a debatable point.
   But _____ that Singapore is an interesting place.

**B** | With a partner, practice the sentences in exercise **A**. Replace the responses with other expressions from the box that have the same meaning.

**C** | Work with your partner. Read the statements below about different urban challenges. Do you agree or disagree with each statement? Discuss your ideas with your partner.

> There should be a $200 fine for using a cell phone while driving.

> I agree. I think there should also be a fine for text messaging while driving.

1. It is the government's responsibility to provide free housing for homeless people.
2. Billboards by the side of the road are ugly and distracting. They should be illegal.
3. Pets should be allowed in restaurants, shops, and movie theaters.
4. Everyone should be allowed to own firearms.
5. Smoking should be prohibited in all public places, both indoors and outdoors.
6. It is impossible for people from different ethnic groups to live together in peace.
7. In crowded cities, the government has the right to limit the number of cars a family can have.

# Grammar

## Using an Agent in Passive Voice Sentences

In passive voice sentences, the agent of the action is not mentioned when:

- The agent is understood and would be redundant.
  *The garbage hasn't been collected yet.* (Agent: *by the garbage collectors*)

- The agent is unknown.
  *A policeman was shot yesterday.*

- The speaker doesn't want to state the agent.
  *The president admitted that mistakes were made.*

You should include the agent in passive sentences when it is important that people know the "doer" of the action. In these types of sentences, the agent follows the word *by*.
*Grass has been planted* **by volunteers** *in all the public parks.*

**A** | Read the paragraph. Circle the passive voice verb forms. Underline any agents.

### Cleaning Up Europe's Urban Rivers

Keeping rivers clean is a challenge for most large cities. In the 1900s, rivers in many cities were polluted by harmful chemicals and raw sewage from nearby industries. Fish were often missing from urban rivers completely. Today, some large European cities are successfully keeping their rivers clean. More and more, fishermen are catching fish in rivers flowing through cities such as London, Paris, and Stockholm. Even fish that require very clean water to live, such as salmon and trout, are being caught. Why are the fish returning? A couple of reasons have been suggested. One reason is the disappearance of industries that used to pollute the rivers. Tough new pollution laws and water rules have also helped make rivers cleaner. Not all the rivers have been cleaned up, but the signs of recovery are promising for Europe's urban rivers.

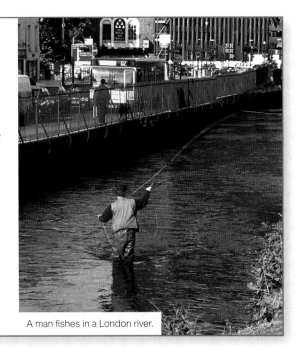
A man fishes in a London river.

 **B** | With a partner, review your answers in exercise **A**. Locate sentences where the passive voice is used without an agent. Why hasn't an agent been used? Decide on a reason.

 **C** | **Discussion.** Select a tourist attraction or landmark in your favorite city. Form a group with two or three other students. Tell the members of your group about this place. Use the passive voice as appropriate. Answer the following questions:

- Where is this place or attraction?
- When was it designed and built?
- What is it used for?
- Will it be changed in the future? How?

In this presentation, you and a partner will present a problem affecting your city and propose solutions to the problem. You and your partner will use a graphic organizer to help organize your ideas.

**A** | With a partner, discuss problems affecting your city. Use your own knowledge and experience. If necessary, look at a local newspaper for information about local problems.

**B** | **Using a Graphic Organizer.** With your partner, choose one of the problems you discussed in exercise **A**. Create a Spider Map like the one below to help you organize your ideas. Write the problem in the center circle of the Spider Map. Discuss the causes of the problem and list them in the Spider Map. Then discuss different ways to solve each problem and add the solutions to the Spider Map. (*See page 214 of the Independent Student Handbook for more information about using graphic organizers.*)

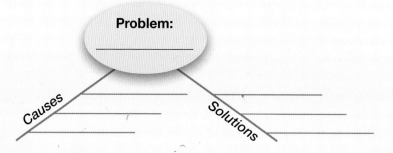

**C** | **Planning a Presentation.** Decide who will present each part of the presentation and practice out loud. Try to include new vocabulary from this unit and the passive voice.

**D** | **Presentation.** With your partner, present your problem and solutions to the class.

> We would like to talk about the problem of youth gangs. The causes are quite complicated. To begin with . . .

> One way to solve this problem is to start an after-school program at the Community Center.

## Presentation Skills: Making Eye Contact

When you are giving a presentation, it is important to make eye contact with the audience. Try to make eye contact a natural part of your presentation. If you are using notes during your presentation, do not read directly from your notes. Instead, look down only when you need help to remember your next point. Look around the room at your listeners and make eye contact with the individuals in the audience.

# Protecting Our Planet

UNIT

2

## Think and Discuss

1. Look at the photo and read the caption. What do you imagine this scene looked like 50 or 60 years ago? What caused the change?
2. What are some reasons that animals become extinct?
3. Who do you think should be responsible for protecting endangered species? Governments? Companies? Citizens?

An endangered turtle floats over a dead coral reef.

# Exploring the Theme:
## Protecting Our Planet

A | Look at the photos and read the caption. Then discuss the questions.

1. Lions and other types of big cats are dying at a rapid rate. What do you think is the biggest threat to these animals?
2. If a plant species becomes extinct, what effect does this have on the environment?

B | Look at the chart. Then discuss the questions.

1. Which group is the most threatened? Which is the least?
2. Which categories of species are common in your country?

## Protecting Our Plants and Animals

Around the planet, human impact has resulted in the destruction of animal and plant life. Now conservationists are trying to save these plants and animals from extinction. Once a plant or animal is extinct, there will be no living members of that species left on the planet.

## Percentage of Threatened Species by Category

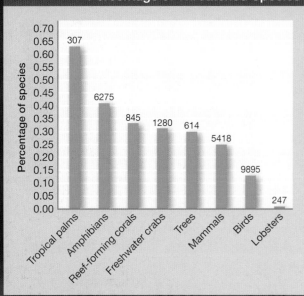

Each year, The International Union for Conservation of Nature studies plants and animals. Many of the species studied are threatened or at risk of dying. The graph shows the percentage of threatened species in each category. The numbers at the top of the graph show how many species were studied.

An African lion rests near a tree in Botswana. Over the past 20 years, nearly 30 percent of all African lions have died.

**A | Meaning from Context.** Read and listen to the information about saving the whales. Notice the words in blue. These are words you will hear and use in Lesson A.

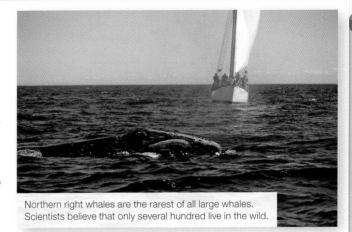

Northern right whales are the rarest of all large whales. Scientists believe that only several hundred live in the wild.

## Save the Whales!

Of the 70 species of whales and dolphins, nearly all have been affected by human activities.

**Does that mean that all whales are endangered?**

Not all, but many. Most species of baleen[1] whales, such as blue and humpback whales, have been significantly reduced. Their status today is the result of commercial whaling in the 19th and 20th centuries, when whales were exploited for meat and oil. Of the eleven baleen species, nine are currently endangered. We have evidence that many toothed whales are also in danger of dying. Threats to whales include hunting, habitat[2] destruction, and pollution.

**What kinds of conservation efforts are taking place?**

Many ongoing conservation strategies are helping whale populations. For example, the International Whaling Commission (IWC) ordered a stop to commercial whaling. Unfortunately, a number of countries have chosen to violate the rule and continue to kill whales.

**Can whale populations recover?**

Although it may be too late for some species, there are some indications that conservation efforts are working. For example, the California gray whale, which was near extinction, has made an amazing recovery. Gray whales were removed from the Endangered Species List.

**How can I help save the whales?**

You can help by learning about whales and their habitats. Donate your time to conservation organizations, and alter your behavior so that you create as little waste as possible. If we all participate in these efforts, we can help protect these magnificent animals.

[1] Instead of having teeth, **baleen** whales have plates in their mouths that separate food from the water.
[2] The **habitat** of an animal or plant is the natural environment in which it lives and grows.

**B | Work with a partner. Match each word in blue from exercise A with its definition.**

1. status (n.) ____
2. exploited (v.) ____
3. threats (n.) ____
4. ongoing (adj.) ____
5. strategies (n.) ____
6. violate (v.) ____
7. recover (v.) ____
8. indications (n.) ____
9. alter (v.) ____
10. evidence (n.) ____

a. plans to achieve a goal, over a long period
b. continuing to happen
c. a state or condition at a particular time
d. signs that something will happen or is true
e. to get stronger and return to an earlier, healthy state
f. facts or physical signs that prove something is true
g. situations or activities that could cause harm or danger
h. to do the opposite of an agreement or law
i. developed or profited from (e.g., resources)
j. to change

**A | Using a Dictionary.** Complete the chart with the correct form of each word. Use your dictionary to help you.

|    | Noun | Verb | Adjective |
|----|------|------|-----------|
| 1. |      | exploit |        |
| 2. | threat |    |           |
| 3. |      | recover |        |
| 4. | indication |  |         |

**B |** Read the article and fill in each blank with the correct form of a word from exercise **A** on page 24.

## Satellite Photos Reveal Damaged Mangrove Forests
by Staff Writers

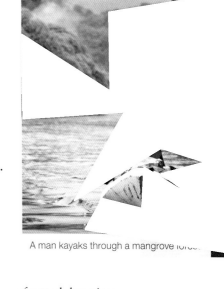

A man kayaks through a mangrove forest

WASHINGTON, D.C.— A recent study by the U.S. Geological Survey shows that mangrove forests cover much less land than previously believed. The research team led by Chandra Giri used more than 1000 satellite images to examine the (1) _____ of mangrove forests worldwide. Giri's team discovered that mangrove forests cover 12 percent less land than previously estimated by the United Nations Food and Agriculture Organization.

(2) _____ from satellite photos (3) _____ that these important coastal forests are disappearing. Mangrove forests are found along the coastlines of 118 different tropical countries. These forests, which consist of trees, shrubs, and palms, protect coastlines and villages against hurricanes and tsunamis, and provide a habitat for many types of ocean wildlife. Human (4) _____ of wood, housing construction, and shrimp farming have all contributed to the destruction of many mangrove forests. Only about seven percent of mangrove forests worldwide are protected by law.

(5) _____ efforts are required to help mangrove forests (6) _____. Recommended (7) _____ include replanting trees, passing laws to protect endangered forests, and forcing individuals or companies that (8) _____ the law to pay fines. Educating citizens, teachers, and public officials about the importance of conservation is also a key step in protecting mangrove forests.

**C | Discussion.** With a partner, discuss the questions.

1. Do you agree that people who alter or destroy mangrove forests should pay a fine? Explain.
2. How can you participate in the efforts to save endangered plants and animals?
3. Which is more important: saving mangrove forests or helping businesses that destroy mangrove forests but help the local economy? Explain.

# Before Listening

**A** | **Predicting Content.** Form a group with two or three other students. Look at the photos and read the caption. Then discuss the questions.

The dusky seaside sparrow was a bird species of southern Florida.

1. What kind of habitat do you think this bird lived in?
2. The dusky seaside sparrow is now extinct. What do you think are some possible causes for its extinction?

---

**Note-Taking**

People generally speak more quickly than they can write. To take good notes quickly while listening to a lecture, write only the most important ideas.

- Write only the key words.
- Don't write complete sentences.
- Use abbreviations (short forms) and symbols when possible.
- Indent specific information, such as examples.

---

track **1-12** **B** | Listen to the first part of a guided tour and look at the student's notes below. Notice the use of key words, indentation, abbreviations, and symbols.

Dusky Seaside Sparrow

Status: Extinct

Former habitat: Merritt Island, FL

Causes of extinction:
1. Chems. used for killing mosquitoes
2. Altered wetlands ⟶ no longer a good habitat
   for sparrows

**C** | Work with a partner. Using the notes from exercise **B**, retell the first part of the lecture in complete sentences. Use your own words.

## Listening: A Guided Tour

track 1-13 **Note-Taking.** Listen to the guided tour and complete the notes. Be sure to use key words, abbreviations, and symbols. Notice the indentations. Listen again if necessary. (*See page 206 of the Independent Student Handbook for more information on taking notes.*)

Endangered Species Act (ESA) - 1973

    Protects animals and their _____

        Ex.: _____

    Ongoing conflict between _____ and _____

        Ex.: _____

    ESA protects _____; ranchers feel law violates _____

Endangered Species Today

    Situation today is _____ than in 1973

    1. _____ species listed as _____ or _____

    2. Since 1973 only _____ species removed from list

    3. BUT only _____ removed because they recovered;

        _____ became extinct, others listed by accident

    4. _____ more species may soon be added to list

Conclusion

    Even w/ ESA in place, _____

## After Listening

**A** | Use your notes from above to answer the questions.

1. What is the main topic of the talk?
   a. Why the dusky seaside sparrow became extinct
   b. The difficulties of protecting both animals and their habitats
   c. Reasons that the Endangered Species Act isn't working
2. What does the Endangered Species Act protect?
   a. Endangered animals and their habitats
   b. Endangered animals but not their habitats
   c. Animal habitats but not endangered animals
3. What has happened since the passage of the Endangered Species Act?
   a. The number of species that are endangered has decreased.
   b. There is more cooperation between landowners and the government.
   c. The number of species that are endangered has stayed the same.

**B** | **Discussion.** Work with a partner. How might the extinction of the dusky seaside sparrow have been prevented? Explain your ideas.

# Language Function

## Introducing Examples

We use many expressions to introduce examples. Most of them are placed directly before the example.

> I've visited many national parks, **for example,** Yellowstone and Yosemite.
> There's a wide variety of animals there—**for instance,** bison and wolves.

> Alligators thrive in habitats **such as** the Everglades swamp.
> The Everglades is home to many species of wildlife, **including** the Florida panther and the American alligator.

A few expressions may be placed after the examples, especially in casual speech.

> I've visited many national parks—Yellowstone and Yosemite, **for example.**
> There's a wide variety of animals there—bison and wolves, **for instance.**

 **A** | In the guided tour, the speakers used expressions to introduce examples. Listen and fill in the expressions you hear.

1. That's why the Endangered Species Act, which was passed in the United States in 1973, protects both endangered animals and their habitats. _____, the steelhead trout lives in rivers and streams on the west coast of the United States. . .

2. There's an ongoing conflict between some landowners and the government. Take the case of the gray wolf, _____.

3. Reports on topics _____ habitat loss, deforestation, and overfishing show that the situation for many species is far worse now than it was in 1973.

4. Meanwhile, another 300 species may soon be added to the list, _____ a plant, the Las Vegas buckwheat, and an insect, the Miami blue butterfly.

The Miami blue butterfly

**B** | **Collaboration.** Work with a partner. Each student should choose a different box. Use the information in the boxes to talk about each animal. Create sentences that include a statement and examples. Explain the information to your partner. Use expressions for introducing examples.

**Student A**

| Statements | Examples |
|---|---|
| 1. Bee populations are decreasing in many areas of the world. | China<br>Brazil<br>North America<br>Europe |
| 2. This decrease is caused by a number of factors. | viruses<br>habitat loss<br>climate change |
| 3. It's important to follow strategies to protect bees. | Educate the public about the role of bees.<br>Pay farmers to protect bee habitats.<br>Use nontoxic chemicals. |

**Student B**

| Statements | Examples |
|---|---|
| 1. Many people are afraid of bats, but bats help the environment in important ways. | Bats eat insects that destroy crops.<br>Fruit-eating bats pollinate[1] plants. |
| 2. Human activities threaten bats. | Machines kill bats.<br>Development destroys their habitat.<br>People kill them. |
| 3. We can take steps to help bats survive. | Explain how bats help the environment.<br>Build a bat house (similar to a bird house).<br>Pass laws to protect bats and their habitats. |

[1] To **pollinate** a plant or tree, insects place pollen in the plant or tree so seeds can be made.

**C** | **Self-Reflection.** Complete these sentences with an expression for introducing examples and your own ideas. Then share your sentences with your partner.

1. I plan to travel to many different places _____.
2. I have seen many types of animals _____.
3. I have visited some wonderful museums _____.

# Grammar

## Restrictive Adjective Clauses

We use adjective clauses, also called relative clauses, to modify a noun. There are two types of adjective clauses: restrictive and non-restrictive. Restrictive adjective clauses give information that is essential for identifying the noun.

Adjective clauses start with relative pronouns. *Who, whose, whom,* and *that* are used for people. *Which* and *that* are used for things. A relative pronoun can be the subject or object of its adjective clause. When the relative pronoun is the object of a restrictive adjective clause, it can be omitted.

Sentences with adjective clauses are formed by combining two simple sentences as follows:

**Relative pronoun as subject**

*Chandra Giri is a scientist.* **She** *used satellite images to study mangrove forests.*

*Chandra Giri is a scientist* **who** *used satellite images to study mangrove forests.*

**Relative pronoun as object**

*The meeting was about conservation efforts in national parks. We attended* **it.**

*The meeting* **that** *we attended was about conservation efforts in national parks.*

**A** | Combine the two sentences. Change the second sentence to an adjective clause.

1. The police discovered the body of a deer. It had been killed illegally.

   _____

2. The woman belongs to a bird-watching club. I met her yesterday.

   _____

3. I know a woman. She keeps two tigers as pets.

   _____

4. I think it was a grizzly bear. It tore open all my trash bags.

   _____

5. There are too many people. They don't care about endangered species.

   _____

**B** | **Collaboration.** Complete these sentences with your own ideas. Use adjective clauses. Then discuss your sentences with a partner.

1. I'm fascinated by animals that _____.
2. I enjoyed talking to the person whom/that _____.
3. Let me tell you about the vacation that _____.

# Brainstorming Ideas about Conservation

## Brainstorming

Brainstorming helps us connect ideas and come up with new ideas about a topic.

To brainstorm in a group, follow these steps:

- Assign one group member to be a secretary. The secretary will take notes for the group.
- Choose a topic. Say as many ideas about the topic as you can. Do not stop to organize your thoughts or correct errors. The secretary will write down all of the ideas.
- After you have finished brainstorming, look over the list and add any related ideas that you may have missed.

**A** | **Brainstorming.** Form a group with two or three other students. Look at the list of habitats in the chart. With your group, brainstorm and complete the chart with examples of plants and animals that live in each place. Then brainstorm about the dangers that the plants and animals face in each habitat.

| Habitat | Animals | Dangers |
|---|---|---|
| ice | polar bear, seal, walrus, penguin | |
| desert | | |
| rain forest | | |
| ocean | | |
| Other: _____ | | |

**B** | **Discussion.** Work with your group. Use the brainstorming list from exercise **A**. Have a group discussion about the dangers that plants and animals face in each habitat.

> Melting ice is dangerous for animals in the ice habitat—polar bears, for example.

> And animals in the ice habitat are also hunted for their fur.

# *Crocodiles of* Sri Lanka

## Before Viewing

**A** | **Predicting Content.** Work with a partner. What is the biggest problem for the crocodiles of Sri Lanka? Brainstorm some ideas.

**B** | **Using the Dictionary.** Some words have more than one meaning. With a partner, read these sentences from the video. Notice the words in blue. Then read the definitions. There are two definitions for each word. Match each word with the definition that fits the sentence from the video. Use your dictionary to help you.

_____ 1. The only chance the **mugger** has in the wild is here, in Yala.

     a. a criminal who robs others in public

     b. a crocodile of southern Asia

_____ 2. If they die out here, they're probably gone **for good**.

     a. forever, permanently

     b. so that things will be better

_____ 3. The winner gets the prize—his **pick** of the females.

     a. a sharp, pointed tool

     b. a choice

_____ 4. Muggers have been acting out this **ritual** for more than 100 million years.

     a. a procedure for a religious ceremony

     b. an activity or behavior that happens often

# While Viewing

**A | Note-Taking.** Watch the first two minutes of the video. Complete the notes with words from the box.

| captive | crocodiles | farms | habitat | human | India | mugger |
|---------|------------|-------|---------|-------|-------|--------|

1. Increased _____ populations → less _____ for animals
2. India: big problem for _____
3. Rom Whitaker wants to save the _____ crocodile
4. Indian wetlands are now _____
5. Madras Crocodile Bank—world's largest _____ pop. of muggers
6. Can't let them go—no place for them in _____

**B | Note-Taking.** Watch the next two minutes of the video. Complete the notes with one or two words you hear.

1. Past: wild muggers throughout Indian _____
2. Today: _____ thousand left
3. _____ years ago: wild muggers in Sri Lanka
4. _____ is going to look for them.
5. Yala National Park—world's largest pop. of _____ muggers

Yala National Park, Sri Lanka

**C |** With your partner, discuss your answers to the question in exercise **A** in the Before Viewing section. Were you correct?

**D | Note-Taking.** Watch the rest of the video and take notes. Then use your notes to answer the questions.

1. Rom wants to know if the Yala muggers are thriving. Why can't he find out from other researchers?
2. Why is Rom observing the muggers at night? What is he doing?
3. Do the males spend a lot of time fighting? Why do they fight? Are many of them killed?

# After Viewing

**A | Collaboration.** With a partner, think of four questions you would like to ask Rom Whitaker about the future of the mugger crocodiles.

**B |** Work with a group of two or three students. One student in the group should pretend to be Rom Whitaker. The other students will ask the questions they wrote in exercise **A**. The student playing Rom Whitaker should answer each question as if he or she is Rom Whitaker.

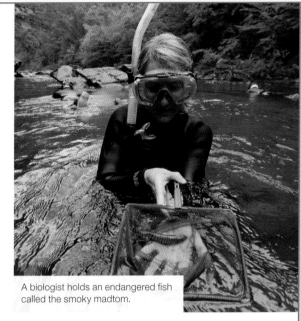

A biologist holds an endangered fish called the smoky madtom.

**A | Meaning from Context.** Read and listen to the interview. Notice the words in blue. These are words you will hear and use in Lesson B.

track 1-15

**Q:** What does a fish biologist do?

**A:** Well, lots of things. I teach at a university and research ways to **maintain** fish populations. I spend a lot of time trying to raise **funds** for research and contacting **authorities** to get permission for the research I want to do. And I get to travel around the world and educate people about **sustainable** fishing.

**Q:** What is the **focus** of your research?

**A:** My interest is to protect large freshwater[1] fish and their habitats. Forty percent of the freshwater fish in North America are in danger of extinction. That's 700 endangered species. And that's just in North America! Each year, when I join other biologists for our **annual** meeting, someone reports on the extinction of another species. That's hard to hear.

**Q:** Don't you get discouraged?

**A:** On the **contrary**, it just makes me want to work harder. I've always loved water, and I've always loved fish. I'm inspired to do what I can to help them survive.

**Q:** If you could tell people to do one thing to help save freshwater fish, what would it be?

**A:** Get involved! **Contribute** as much time as you can. Volunteer to help clean up a river, or write letters to politicians to make them aware of the **issues**. Above all, don't **ignore** the problem, because things are not going to get better without our help.

[1] **Freshwater** lakes and rivers contain water that is not salty.

**B | Using a Dictionary.** Work with a partner. Match each word from exercise **A** with its definition. Use your dictionary to help you.

1. maintain (v.) ____
2. funds (n.) ____
3. authorities (n.) ____
4. sustainable (adj.) ____
5. focus (n.) ____
6. annual (adj.) ____
7. contrary (n.) ____
8. contribute (v.) ____
9. issues (n.) ____
10. ignore (v.) ____

a. important problems that people are discussing or arguing about
b. to give money or time to make an effort successful
c. happening once a year
d. to pay no attention to
e. able to be kept at a certain level without causing damage to the animals or the environment
f. a topic that you are concentrating on or paying special attention to
g. to take care of something and keep it in good condition
h. the opposite of an idea or condition
i. people who have the power to make decisions and to make sure that laws are obeyed
j. amounts of money given to organizations or people to be spent for a purpose

**A** | Read the article and fill in each blank with the correct form of a word from exercise **A** on page 34. Use a dictionary if necessary.

## The Yellowstone Wolf Project

Wolves were once common throughout North America, but by the mid-1930s, most had been killed. In 1995 and 1996, the United States Fish and Wildlife Service (1) _____ a plan to capture wolves from Canada and free them in Yellowstone National Park. This program, known as the Yellowstone Wolf Project, cost only $267,000 in government (2) _____. It was a huge success. Today, the Yellowstone wolf population has recovered and can (3) _____ itself.

Wolves in Yellowstone National Park

(4) _____ to the wishes of many farmers and ranchers, wolf populations have also been recovering in other parts of the western United States. As the number of wolves has grown, wolves have become the (5) _____ of a bitter debate. People cannot (6) _____ the fact that wolves occasionally kill sheep, cattle, and other farm animals. On the other hand, wolves hunt and help control populations of grazing animals such as elk, moose, and deer.

The presence of wolves brings financial benefits to Yellowstone Park. Tens of thousands of tourists visit Yellowstone (7) _____ to see the wolves. Those tourists provide money to help (8) _____ the park and keep it in good condition. Tourists also (9) _____ about 35 million dollars a year to the area around the park. The Yellowstone Wolf Project continues to be a complicated (10) _____ with strong arguments for and against the effort.

**B** | **Critical Thinking.** Form a group with two or three other students and discuss the questions.

1. In many places in the United States, wolves are protected by the Endangered Species Act. If wolf populations have recovered, should wolves continue to be protected by law? Why, or why not?
2. If a wolf attacks a farmer's sheep or cattle, should the farmer have the right to kill the wolf? Explain your opinion.
3. Do you think the government should pay farmers or ranchers whose animals are killed by wolves? Why, or why not?

## Before Listening

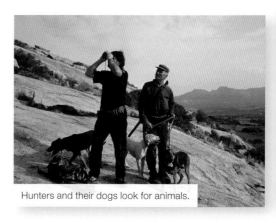

Hunters and their dogs look for animals.

👥 **Prior Knowledge.** With a partner, discuss the questions below.

1. Ducks, quail, turkeys, and pheasants are popular birds to hunt. Elk and deer are popular four-legged animals to hunt. What other animals do you know that are hunted?
2. Have you ever gone hunting? If you have, did you like it? If you haven't, would you like to try it? Explain.

## Listening: A Student Debate

**Critical Thinking Focus: Evaluating Arguments in a Debate**

In a debate, speakers take turns presenting arguments for or arguments against a controversial issue. Each speaker provides facts, examples, and statistics to prove that his or her argument is accurate. Each speaker also tries to show that the other speaker's arguments are incorrect, incomplete, or illogical. Members of the audience must listen and decide which speaker presented a stronger argument.

🎧 track 1-16 **A | Listening for Key Concepts.** Listen to two classmates debate about legalized hunting. Who speaks in favor of it? Who speaks against it?

🎧 track 1-16 **B | Note-Taking.** Listen again. Take notes on the speakers' arguments for and against hunting. Also take notes on their responses to each other's arguments.

| Yumi's Arguments for Hunting | Yumi's Responses to Raoul |
|---|---|
| Hunting helps control animal pops. | |

| Raoul's Arguments against Hunting | Raoul's Responses to Yumi |
|---|---|
| Some hunters are irresponsible. | |

👥 **C |** With a partner, compare your notes from exercise **B**. Restate the arguments for hunting and against hunting in your own words.

👥 **D | Discussion.** Refer back to the debate. Which speaker do you think presented the stronger argument? Explain your opinion to your partner.

# After Listening

**Critical Thinking.** Form a group with two or three other students. Then answer the questions.

1. Do you think that hunting should be allowed in your area? If yes, what hunting rules would you make? If no, why not?
2. Some groups believe that teaching children and teenagers about hunting will make them responsible hunters as adults. Should the government try to convince more young people to take up hunting? Explain your opinion.

# Pronunciation

track 1-17

> **Pronouncing -s endings**
>
> The letter *s* at the end of nouns, verbs, and possessives has three pronunciations. Put your hand on your throat and say *zeeeeeee*. This is a voiced sound, so you should feel a vibration in your throat. Now, put your hand on your throat and say *ssssss*. This is a voiceless sound, so there is no vibration in your throat.
>
> > After voiceless consonants, *s* is pronounced /s/: *duc**ks**, hun**ts**, photograp**hs***
> > After voiced consonants and all vowels, *s* is pronounced /z/: *bea**rs**, be**es**, mangrov**es***
> > After words ending in *ss*, *sh*, *ch*, *ce*, *se*, *ge*, or *x*, *s* is pronounced /ɪz/: *grass**es**, buzz**es**, fish**es**, catch**es***
>
> When a word ending in *s* is followed by a word that starts with a vowel, the two words are linked.
> > *ducks in danger     hunts after dark     bears and deer     dollars annually*

**A** | Look at the following words. How is the final *s* pronounced? Check (✔) your answer.

|  | | /s/ | /z/ | /ɪz/ |  | | | /s/ | /z/ | /ɪz/ |
|---|---|---|---|---|---|---|---|---|---|---|
| 1. | government's | ❏ | ❏ | ❏ | | 5. | elks | ❏ | ❏ | ❏ |
| 2. | hunters | ❏ | ❏ | ❏ | | 6. | boys | ❏ | ❏ | ❏ |
| 3. | crashes | ❏ | ❏ | ❏ | | 7. | stamps | ❏ | ❏ | ❏ |
| 4. | whales | ❏ | ❏ | ❏ | | 8. | passes | ❏ | ❏ | ❏ |

track 1-18

**B** | Listen and check your answers in exercise **A**. Then listen again and repeat the words you hear. Pay special attention to the pronunciation of the final *s*.

track 1-19

**C** | With a partner, practice saying the phrases in the box below. Be careful to link the final *s* sound with the first vowel of the next word. Then listen and check your pronunciation.

| | | | |
|---|---|---|---|
| government's actions | hunters' activities | crashes into | whales ahead |
| elks' antlers | species of birds | stamps in use | passes out |

# Language Function

track 1-20 **A** | In the listening, the classmates used a number of expressions for responding to and refuting an argument. Listen and fill in the expressions you hear.

1. **Yumi:** . . . without hunting, deer populations would be too large, and many animals would starve because there wouldn't be enough food to sustain them.
   **Raoul:** _____, I think you're ignoring an important point.
2. **Raoul:** So instead of allowing humans to hunt, we should allow populations of meat-eating animals to recover.
   **Yumi:** _____ don't forget that wolves and mountain lions don't just eat deer and elk.
3. **Raoul:** And in Shenandoah National Park in Virginia, authorities recently caught a group of hunters who were shooting black bears and selling their body parts for medicines.
   **Yumi:** _____ that these kinds of violations occur. However, they are rare.

 **B** | With a partner, practice the sentences from exercise **A**. Then switch roles and read them again.

**C** | With your partner, take turns reading the statements below. Explain your opinion about each statement. Explain the reasons for your opinion. If you disagree with your partner, use the expressions in the Language Function box to respond to or refute your partner's arguments.

1. Human beings have always been hunters. Hunting and killing animals is natural for us.
2. We should stop fishing for a few years to allow fish populations to recover.
3. Just as humans have rights, I believe animals have rights, too.
4. The government does not have the right to stop people from hunting on their own land.
5. I don't care if the dusky seaside sparrow becomes extinct. It doesn't make any difference in my life.

> Hunting should be illegal because many people are hurt in hunting accidents each year.

> Yes, but more people are hurt in car accidents each year. Does that mean we should make driving illegal, too?

# Grammar

## Non-Restrictive Adjective Clauses

Unlike restrictive adjective clauses, non-restrictive adjective clauses provide extra information about a noun.

Adjective clauses following proper nouns, plural nouns, and unique nouns are typically non-restrictive. For example:

> The largest land animal in North America is the American bison, **which can be over six feet (two meters) tall.** (unique noun)
>
> John Muir, **who lived from 1838 to 1914,** was one of America's earliest conservationists. (proper noun)
>
> Lions, **whose roars can be heard for miles,** are quickly disappearing in the wild. (plural noun)

Often there is a slight pause between a non-restrictive clause and the preceding noun. When you are talking about things, use the pronoun *which.* Do not use *that.*

**A** | Combine the two sentences into one sentence using a non-restrictive adjective clause. Use the relative pronouns *who, which,* or *whose.* Insert commas as needed.

1. The dusky seaside sparrow became extinct due to changes to its habitat. It lived in the wetlands of southern Florida.

   *The dusky seaside sparrow, which lived in the wetlands of southern Florida, became*

   *extinct due to changes to its habitat.*

2. Sting works to protect the Amazon. He is a British celebrity.

   _____

3. Whales were hunted to near extinction. They are the largest animals on earth.

   _____

4. Wolves have been introduced into Yellowstone. It is America's oldest national park.

   _____

5. The hippopotamus is not an endangered species at this time. It lives in African rivers.

   _____

6. Businessman Ted Turner allows elk hunting on his land during part of the year. His ranch is very large.

   _____

**B** | **Collaboration.** With a partner, complete the following sentences. Use a non-restrictive adjective clause and your own information.

1. Not long ago I heard an interesting speaker named _____, who . . .

2. I have a _____ relationship with my neighbors, whose . . .

3. My favorite item, which I bought _____, is . . .

In this section, you will evaluate arguments for and against keeping wild animals in zoos. Then you will organize and prepare for a debate on this question.

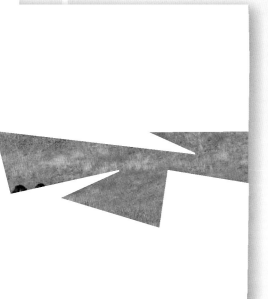

**A** | **Evaluating Arguments.** Read the statements below. Are these arguments for or against keeping animals in zoos? Write **F** if the argument is *for zoos* or **A** if the argument is *against zoos*.

_____ 1. Animals do not have rights, so it is acceptable for people to keep them in zoos.

_____ 2. Zoos educate people about how to protect endangered species.

_____ 3  In many zoos, animals are kept in small cages and cannot move around.

_____ 4. It costs a lot of money to keep animals in zoos.

_____ 5. It is fun to see interesting and unusual animals in zoos.

_____ 6. Zoos protect animals that are hunted illegally, such as rhinos and elephants.

_____ 7. People can be educated about animals without keeping animals in zoos.

_____ 8. The artificial environment of a zoo is very stressful for many animals. They often stop eating.

 **B** | With a partner, take turns reading and responding to the statements in exercise **A**. In your responses, use expressions for responding to and refuting an argument from the box on page 38.

**C** | **Organizing Ideas.** Your teacher will instruct you to prepare arguments for or against keeping animals in zoos. Write down notes to support your position. Try to predict the arguments the other speaker will make, and think of how you will answer them.

**D** | **Presentation.** Your teacher will pair you with a student who prepared the opposite side of the issue. You will hold a three to five minute debate in front of the class or a small group of classmates. The student who speaks in favor of zoos should begin.

**Student to Student:**
**Expressing Encouragement**

Here are some expressions you can use to wish another student good luck before a presentation.

*Good luck!*
*Go for it!*
*Go get 'em!*

**Presentation Skills: Speaking with Confidence**

When speaking in front of a group, it is important to appear confident. This will give the impression that you know your topic well, and that you believe in what you are saying. There are several things that you can do to feel more confident. Make sure you have organized your notes and have practiced your presentation at least once. Use hand gestures and body language when you can. Finally, remember to pause between sentences and to speak slowly and clearly.

# Beauty and Appearance

## Think and Discuss

1. Look at the photo and read the caption. Does this advertisement make you want to buy clothing or beauty products? Explain.

2. How would you describe the items this man is wearing?

3. What surprises or interests you about this photo?

An advertisement for a fashion designer hangs on the side of a building in Milan, Italy.

# Exploring the Theme:
## Beauty and Appearance

A | Look at the photos and read the captions. Then discuss the questions.

1. What makes a person beautiful, in your opinion?
2. Do different people and cultures have different ideas about what is beautiful? Give some examples.

B | Look at the chart. Then discuss the questions.

1. Does it surprise you to find these five countries in the chart? Explain.
2. What country do you think would be next on the chart?

### What is Beauty?

How much of a person's beauty is based on physical appearance? How much depends on what people wear or where they live? Some people go to spas to make themselves beautiful while others dress in unusual fashions. People around the world have different ideas about what makes someone beautiful.

Colorful jewelry and sandals are for sale at an outdoor stand in Colombia.

**A** | Read the paragraph and fill in each blank with the correct form of a word from the box.

classic        constitute        disturb        envision        evolve

Have you ever considered cosmetic surgery? The idea of changing one's looks surgically (1) _____ or even frightens many people. Still, people's feelings about cosmetic surgery have (2) _____ over time. According to the International Society of Aesthetic Plastic Surgeons,[1] more than 8 million cosmetic surgeries were completed worldwide in 2009. The most popular type of cosmetic surgery was liposuction, a surgery where fat is removed from the body. Liposuction surgeries (3) _____ about 19 percent of the total cosmetic surgeries in the world.

With modern cosmetic surgery, you (4) _____ what you want to look like and then use surgery to make it happen. For example, think about the (5) _____ beauties of the movies. Would you like Marilyn Monroe's nose, Audrey Hepburn's eyes, or Grace Kelly's chin? They can be yours—for a price. The average price for liposuction is nearly $3000 and a hair transplant may cost more than $4500. No one ever said beauty was cheap!

A doctor marks a woman's face before she has cosmetic surgery.

[1]**Aesthetic plastic surgery** is another way to refer to cosmetic surgery.

**B** | **Self-Reflection.** Form a group with two or three other students and discuss the questions.

1. What is your perception of cosmetic surgery? Explain your opinion.
2. Determine the ratio of men to women in your class or at your workplace.
3. Would you prefer to live in a city where the weather changes often or in a city where the weather is always consistent? Explain your answer.
4. Have you ever had a random meeting with a person who later became your friend? Talk about how you met.
5. Do you like to follow the same schedule every day or do you prefer a variation of your daily activities? Explain your answer.

# Before Listening

**Discussion.** With a partner, discuss the questions.

1. Look at the two rows of photos. These photos were shown to people who participated in a study on beauty. In each row, select the photo that shows the most beautiful face, in your opinion. Do you and your partner agree?

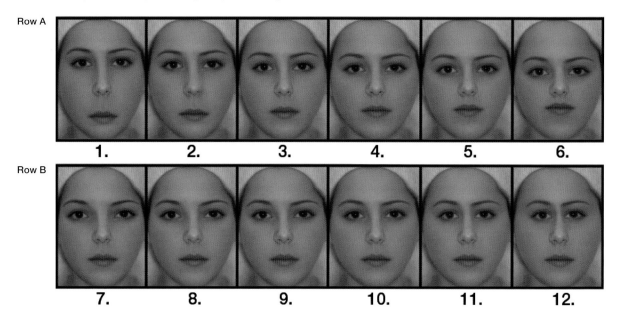

Row A
1.     2.     3.     4.     5.     6.

Row B
7.     8.     9.     10.     11.     12.

2. Look at the photos again. According to researchers, most people would choose Photo 4 and Photo 9 as the most beautiful faces. Did you choose these photos? Explain.

## Listening: A News Report

**A | Listening for Main Ideas.** Listen to a news report about beauty. Match each scientist or group of scientists with the correct research results.

track 1-22

| Scientists | Research Results |
|---|---|
| 1. Judith Langlois ＿＿ | a. Men's ideas about beauty and attractiveness evolved over thousands of years. |
| 2. Pamela M. Pallett<br>Stephen Link<br>Kang Lee ＿＿ | b. Symmetry is a key part of what makes a face beautiful. |
| 3. Victor Johnston<br>David Perrett ＿＿ | c. There is a "golden ratio" for the ideal distance between the eyes, the mouth, and the edge of the face. |
| 4. Don Symons ＿＿ | d. Men prefer large eyes, full lips, and a small nose and chin. |

**B | Listening for Details.** Listen again and circle the correct answer to each question or statement.

1. According to the research, most people think that a beautiful face is _____.
   a. a face with small eyes
   b. average and almost symmetrical
   c. disturbing to observers

2. The "golden ratio" for the length of a face states that the distance between the eyes and the mouth _____.
   a. is 36 percent of the length of the whole face
   b. is 56 percent of the length of the whole face
   c. is 66 percent of the length of the whole face

3. What facial features did scientists Victor Johnston and David Perrett think men find most beautiful?
   a. blue eyes, full lips, and a strong chin
   b. large eyes, full lips, and a small chin
   c. large eyes, thin lips, and a strong nose

4. What conclusion does the reporter, Gwen Silva, probably agree with?
   a. Beauty is in the eye of the beholder.
   b. There is no variation in the ideas about beauty between cultures.
   c. People from the same culture mostly agree on what makes someone beautiful.

## After Listening

**Critical Thinking.** Form a group with two or three other students and discuss the questions.

1. Do you agree or disagree with the saying "Beauty is in the eye of the beholder"? Explain your opinions.
2. Scientists believe that a beautiful face is a symmetrical face. What other features make a face beautiful to you?
3. The news report said that perceptions of beauty vary from culture to culture. Can you give any examples of how perceptions of beauty vary between cultures?

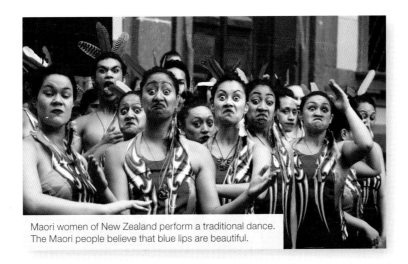

Maori women of New Zealand perform a traditional dance. The Maori people believe that blue lips are beautiful.

# Language Function

## Paraphrasing

During lectures and conversations, speakers often need to paraphrase information. If you paraphrase, you express what was said in a different way. Paraphrasing is a useful way to restate information that may be new or difficult for listeners to understand. Here are some expressions you can use to paraphrase information.

*I mean . . .*                                 *Let me put it another way.*
*In other words . . .*                     *To put it another way . . .*
*That is (to say), . . .*

**A** | In the news report, there were a number of useful expressions for paraphrasing. Listen to the sentences from the news report and fill in the expressions.

track 1-23

1. An often-quoted expression is "Beauty is only skin deep." _____, someone can be beautiful on the outside, but be mean or unpleasant on the inside.

2. Another famous saying is "Beauty is in the eye of the beholder." _____, each person's idea of beauty is different.

3. In addition, the research shows that a beautiful face is a symmetrical face. _____, if both sides of the face are exactly the same, we consider a person beautiful.

## Critical Thinking Focus: Understanding Quotations

Speakers sometimes use quotations when talking with others. A quotation is a sentence or phrase from another speaker that you repeat in your own speech. Quotations are often used to introduce the topic of a lecture, to emphasize an idea, or to end a conversation in an interesting way.

**B** | Read these quotations about beauty. In your own words, write what each quotation means.

1. Beauty is not in the face; beauty is a light in the heart. —Kahlil Gibran

_____

2. It matters more what's in a woman's face than what's on it. —Claudette Colbert

_____

3. I've never seen a smiling face that was not beautiful. —Author Unknown

_____

4. Time is a great healer, but a poor beautician.[1] —Lucille S. Harper

_____

[1]A **beautician** is a person who cuts hair and performs other beauty-related tasks for people.

**C | Paraphrasing.** Work with a partner. Take turns reading the quotations in exercise **B** on page 48. Explain each quotation to your partner using a paraphrasing expression.

> Beauty is not in the face; beauty is a light in the heart. In other words, a person's beauty doesn't come from the way they look. It comes from their personality.

## Grammar

### Compound Adjectives

Compound adjectives are made up of two words, but act as a single idea. Compound adjectives are used to modify nouns. Compound adjectives can be formed in many different ways.

| Adjective + past participle | Adverb + past participle | Noun + past participle |
|---|---|---|
| a **kind-hearted** man | a **highly respected** firm | a **sun-dried** tomato |
| a **red-headed** assistant | **consistently applied** rules | a **sweat-soaked** shirt |

**A** | Study the grammar box above. Then look at the words in the boxes below. With a partner, come up with a compound adjective that describes each noun. Choose one word from each box to form the compound adjective.

**Box A**

| good | often | rose |
|---|---|---|
| highly | poorly | sugar |

**Box B**

| built | free | motivated |
|---|---|---|
| colored | looking | quoted |

a red-headed office worker

1. a _____ structure
2. a(n) _____ saying
3. _____ students
4. _____ glasses
5. a _____ cake
6. a _____ model

**B** | Work with your partner. One student will be Student A and the other will be Student B. Read each sentence in your list to your partner. Your partner will restate the sentence using a compound adjective.

I see a girl with brown eyes.

I see a brown-eyed girl.

## Student A

1. I have an interview for a job that is part time.
2. The chef is preparing a meal that makes my mouth water.
3. I gave Elena the vase that was made by hand.
4. I can't wear this shirt that is soaked with sweat.

## Student B

5. I'm going to buy a bookshelf that is four feet tall.
6. If you are a person who looks good, you might be able to have a career as a model.
7. The author who is world famous is visiting my university.
8. In an emergency, it's good to know that the babysitter has a cool head.

**C** | **Discussion.** Form a group with two or three other students and discuss the questions. Try to use compound adjectives.

1. What are some world-famous companies that you can think of?
2. Who is the most highly-respected person you know?
3. What is an often-quoted saying from your language? Do you agree with the saying?
4. What are some time-saving tips for helping to complete errands? Share your ideas with your group.
5. What are some well-known magazines and newspapers in your area?

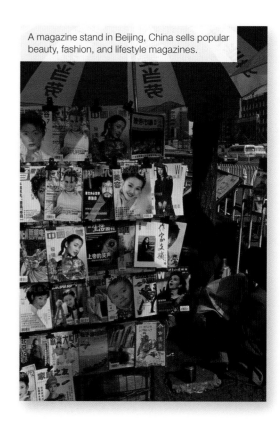

A magazine stand in Beijing, China sells popular beauty, fashion, and lifestyle magazines.

# Conducting a Survey

**A** | Follow the instructions to conduct a survey of your classmates' ideas about beauty.

1. Choose four of the following questions to include in your survey. Then write two new questions of your own.

> **Survey Questions**
> - Is it better to be beautiful, intelligent, or wealthy? Explain your choice.
> - Who do you think is the most beautiful woman alive today? Who is the most handsome man alive today?
> - What is the minimum age at which people should be allowed to have cosmetic surgery?
> - What is the most unusual item of clothing you own?
> - What do you spend more money on: clothing and beauty supplies, food, or electronics?
> - Are there any fashions today that you think are strange?

2. On a piece of paper, make a chart similar to the one below. Write your questions.

| Questions | Student 1: | Student 2: | Student 3: |
|---|---|---|---|
| What is the most unusual item of clothing you own? | | | |

3. Talk to three of your classmates. Ask each classmate the survey questions you have chosen. In your notebook, take notes on each person's answers.

**B** | Form a group with two or three other students. Discuss the survey results. What is interesting or surprising about the information you heard? How would you answer each question in the survey? Discuss your thoughts with your group.

> The people that I surveyed think being intelligent is more important than being beautiful or wealthy. I agree with that.

## Student to Student: Asking about Personal Opinions

Asking about a person's opinion can help you learn more information about that person. Here are some expressions you can use to ask about personal opinions.

*What about you? What do you think?*
*What was your experience like?*

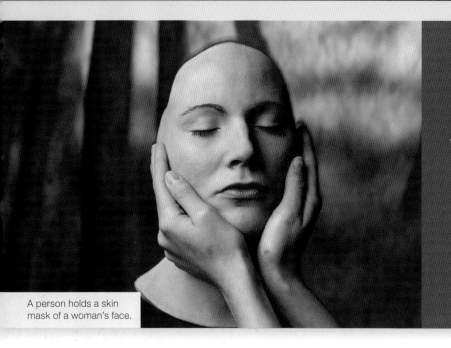

A person holds a skin mask of a woman's face.

# Skin Mask

## Before Viewing

**A** | **Using a Dictionary.** Look at the words in the box. You will hear these words and phrases in the video. Write each word or phrase from the box next to the correct definition. Use your dictionary to help you.

| gooey | inject | mummy | silicone | special effects |
|-------|--------|-------|----------|-----------------|

1. _____ (n.) a rubber-like material
2. _____ (adj.) soft and sticky
3. _____ (n.) a dead body wrapped in cloth as in ancient Egyptian tombs
4. _____ (n.) in movies, unusual images or sounds created using special techniques
5. _____ (v.) to force a liquid into something

**B** | **Predicting Content.** Look at the photos on pages 52 and 53 and read the captions. How do you think a skin mask is made? Discuss your ideas with the class.

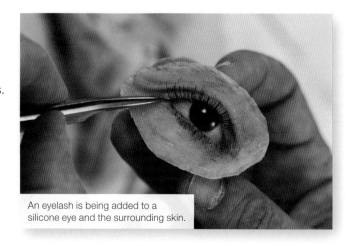

An eyelash is being added to a silicone eye and the surrounding skin.

# While Viewing

**A** | Watch the video and choose the correct answer to each question.

1. Where are the people in the video?
   a. They are in a hospital.
   b. They are in a special-effects studio.
   c. They are in a room in Mike's home.

2. Why does the narrator say that Cassandra is brave?
   a. Because modeling for the skin mask is uncomfortable.
   b. Because she had cosmetic surgery on her face.
   c. Because she is the first model for a new type of skin mask.

3. How will the skin mask likely be used?
   a. To fool Cassandra's friends
   b. To demonstrate cosmetic surgery
   c. For special effects in a movie

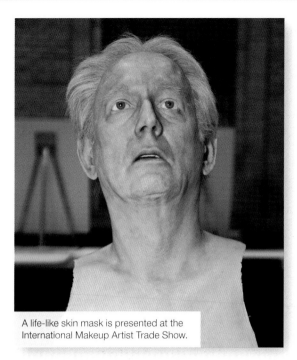

A life-like skin mask is presented at the International Makeup Artist Trade Show.

**B** | **Sequencing Events.** Watch the video again. Put the steps for making a skin mask in the correct order from 1 to 9.

_____ a. The artists create a series of positive and negative masks.

_____ b. The mixture is injected into the master mold.

__1__ c. A cap is placed on Cassandra's hair.

_____ d. Her face is wrapped in bandages.

_____ e. The artists mix soft silicone and then color it with chemicals.

_____ f. Vaseline is brushed over her eyebrows and eyelashes.

_____ g. Makeup, eyebrows, and eyelashes are added to the skin mask.

_____ h. The hardened material comes off.

_____ i. Artists paint her face in quick-drying silicone.

# After Viewing

**Critical Thinking.** With a partner, discuss the questions.

1. This skin mask is made by special-effects artists. How do you think a skin mask might be used for special effects in movies?

2. What are some other ways a skin mask could be used?

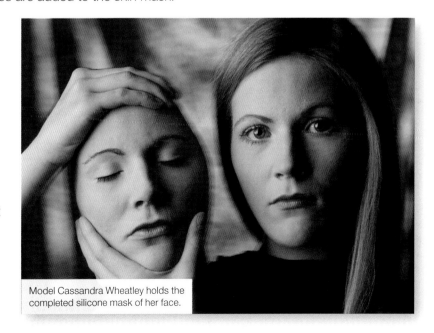

Model Cassandra Wheatley holds the completed silicone mask of her face.

track 1-24 **A** | **Using a Dictionary.** Read the sentences. Write the word from the box that can replace each word in parentheses. These are words you will hear and use in Lesson B. Use your dictionary to help you. Then listen and check your answers.

| | | | | |
|---|---|---|---|---|
| alternative | convince | derive | insert | textile |
| considerably | definite | exhibit | integrate | transport |

1. Joanne tried to _____ (persuade) Steven to enter his design in the fashion show.

2. Eco-fashion is a(n) _____ (different) type of fashion that uses recycled materials.

3. The artist is going to _____ (display) her latest work at a museum in Barcelona.

4. The workers in that _____ (fabric) factory are treated fairly and paid well.

5. To sew the dress, _____ (put) the needle into the fabric and make small stitches.

6. You can _____ (make) a light, smooth fabric called rayon from plant cells.

7. The architect will _____ (combine) traditional and modern elements in the building he is designing.

8. My new job as a nurse pays _____ (a lot) more than my old job as an office worker.

9. They will _____ (move) the trees to the park by truck.

10. The fashion show will be sometime in May, but the exact date is not yet _____ (certain).

**B** | Read the information about eco-fashion. Fill in each blank with the correct form of a word from exercise **A**.

**Q:** What is eco-fashion?

**A:** Eco-fashion is all about making and wearing clothing that is safe and healthy for the environment, shoppers, and workers in the fashion industry. For example, some eco-fashion designers do not think clothes should be (1) _____ long distances in trucks that use gasoline and create air pollution.

**Q:** Are eco-fashions made from traditional (2) _____ such as cotton?

**A:** Not always. Some eco-fashions combine or (3) _____ recycled or reused materials such as second-hand[1] clothes. Some fibers used in eco-fashion are even (4) _____ from plastic bottles.

**Q:** What do eco-fashions look like?

**A:** Eco-fashion is very innovative! In fact, you might think that some of the most imaginative eco-fashion ideas are strange. At a recent eco-fashion show, designers (5) _____ several new designs that used real plants. The designs included a ring with grass growing from it, a shirt collar made of living moss, and a handbag with a space in the center into which you can (6) _____ a plant.

[1]**Second-hand** items are not new and have been owned by someone else.

The caption for the image reads: "This eco-fashion dress is made from recycled light bulbs."

**A** | Use the correct form of each word from the box to complete the information. Use each word only once.

| alternative | convince | considerably | exhibit | insert | integrate | transport |

If you don't already think clothing and textiles are amazing, here are a few examples that will (1) _____ you that they truly are.

The Cargolifter balloon can lift up to 75 tons.

- The Cargolifter is a fabric balloon that is (2) _____ taller than most ballons. It is nearly as tall as a 20-story building. It can carry up to 75 tons. It is used to (3) _____ trains from one place to another.

- A design laboratory has developed an "intelligent apron" that can understand what you say and help you in the kitchen. Electronics and a microphone are (4) _____ into the apron. The apron can turn on the stove, set a cooking timer, or show you a recipe on a screen.

- New York City's Museum of Modern Art recently (5) _____ a number of (6) _____ items. One was "non-stop shoes." These shoes collect the energy you create in the day, and in the evening you can (7) _____ an electric cord into them to power your electronic devices.

## Understanding Suffixes

A suffix is placed at the end of a word in order to form a different word. The suffixes -ive or -ative are often added to words to form adjectives. It is often necessary to drop the final letter of the verb before you add a suffix.

*imagine*   Do you prefer traditional fashion designs or **imaginative** ones?

**B** | **Using a Dictionary.** Use a verb from the box below and the suffix -ive or -ative to complete the sentences. Use your dictionary to help you. (See page 209 of the Independent Student Handbook for more information on suffixes.)

| act | addict | construct | cooperate | definite | derive |

1. _____ learning is when students do coursework together.
2. We need to set a _____ date for our wedding.
3. Caffeine and nicotine are two _____ substances.
4. A person who does a lot of exercise has a(n) _____ lifestyle.
5. Criticism that is meant to help someone to improve is called _____ criticism.
6. _____ art is unoriginal; it copies elements from other artists' work.

# Before Listening

👥 **Predicting Content.** You are going to listen to three people talking about unusual fashions. Look at the photos. What do you think these items are? Discuss your ideas with a partner.

1. _____     2. _____     3. _____

# Listening: An Informal Conversation

track 1-25 **A |** **Listening for Main Ideas.** Listen to the conversation. Look back at the photos. Under each photo, write the name or a brief description of the item.

track 1-25 **B |** **Note-Taking.** Listen again and complete the notes. (*See page 206 of the Independent Student Handbook for more information on note-taking.*)

Antigravity jacket: part _____ and part _____

Kevlar: _____ fiber, stronger than _____

• used in _____ and _____

• developed in _____

Biosteel made from _____ protein produced in _____

• possible uses: _____

Wearable electronics integrate _____ and _____

• Ex.: GPS sneakers allow parents to _____

track 1-25

**C | Listening for Specific Information.** Listen again. With a partner, answer the questions.

1. According to the conversation, where does Danish clothing designer Alex Soza get his ideas?
2. Which piece of clothing was modeled at the fashion show by an animal?
3. Why can't textile manufacturers raise large groups of spiders?
4. What does the man think about the future of wearable technology?

## After Listening

**Critical Thinking.** With a partner, discuss the questions.

1. What are some uses for an antigravity jacket?
2. Goats and spiders are used in the production of Biosteel. Do you think it is acceptable to use animals for the purpose of creating new textiles? Explain your answer.
3. What could be some additional uses of GPS sneakers, besides helping parents to track their children?
4. Ten years from now, what other types of wearable electronics could people be wearing?

## Pronunciation

> **Pronouncing /ŋ/ and /ŋk/**
>
> The /ŋ/ sound is often spelled with the letters *ng*.
>
> /ŋ/        so**ng**, walk**ing**, ri**ng**
>
> The sound /ŋk/ is usually spelled *nc* or *nk*.
>
> /ŋk/        u**nc**le, a**nk**le

track 1-26

**A |** Listen again to the words from the box and repeat the words after the speaker.

**B | Collaboration.** Work with a partner. Brainstorm words that have the /ŋ/ or /ŋk/ sound. Then write three questions using words from the pronunciation box or from your list. Take turns asking and answering your questions with your partner. Focus on the correct pronunciation of /ŋ/ and /ŋk/

Do you have any uncles?

Yes, I have three uncles.

What are their names?

# Language Function

**A** | In the conversation, the speakers use a number of expressions to ask for clarification. Listen to the sentences and fill in the missing expressions.

track 1-27

1. **Sandra:** That antigravity jacket was like a piece of science fiction.

   **Ana:** Antigravity jacket? _____ an antigravity jacket?

2. **David:** That jacket was interesting, I guess. But what amazed me was the vest made of Kevlar.

   **Ana:** _____ Kevlar _____?

3. **Ana:** Well, my friend was exhibiting some of her designs at an art gallery downtown, so I went there. She designs wearable electronics.

   **Sandra:** _____ wearable electronics?

**B** | Work with a partner. One student is Student A and the other is Student B. Your partner will read aloud a statement which includes an unknown word. Ask your partner for clarification about the word. Your partner will locate the definition from the box below and give you more information.

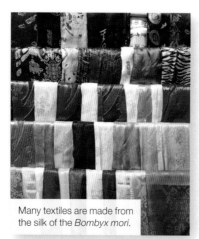

Many textiles are made from the silk of the *Bombyx mori*.

What is *Bombyx mori*?

*Bombyx mori* is the scientific name of the silk worm.

### Student A

1. Next week Marjan is going to have **rhinoplasty**.
2. It cost 2 million dollars to develop a **prototype** of the electronic shoes.

### Student B

3. I would never wear clothing made from spider webs because I have **arachnophobia**.
4. By law, children's pajamas must be **noncombustible**.

### Definitions

**Rhinoplasty** is surgery to change the shape of the nose.
A **prototype** is the first model of a new product.
**Arachnophobia** is a great fear of spiders.
**Noncombustible** materials do not burn.

# Grammar

## Tag Questions

Tag questions help keep a conversation going. Tag questions are formed by adding a short question (or "tag") to the end of a statement. Affirmative statements have negative tags, and negative statements have affirmative tags. A listener can respond to tag questions by agreeing or disagreeing.

| Questions | Responses | |
|---|---|---|
| *That's a very interesting dress, **isn't it**?* | *Yes, **it is**.* | *No, **it isn't**.* |
| *She wasn't thinking about becoming a fashion designer, **was she**?* | *Yes, **she was**.* | *No, **she wasn't**.* |
| *You haven't worn that before, **have you**?* | *Yes, **I have**.* | *No, **I haven't**.* |
| *This fabric won't tear easily, **will it**?* | *Yes, **it will**.* | *No, **it won't**.* |

**A** | With a partner, complete the conversations with tag questions and appropriate answers. Then take turns asking and answering each question.

1. **Q:** Alex Soza is a very imaginative clothing designer, isn't he?
   **A:** Yes, he is _____.

2. **Q:** We've already discussed eco-fashion, _____?
   **A:** Yes, _____.

3. **Q:** You'd like to learn more about wearable electronics, _____?
   **A:** No, _____.

4. **Q:** You're not going to wear a wool sweater today, _____?
   **A:** Yes, _____.

5. **Q:** It's not possible to make textiles from plastic bottles, _____?
   **A:** Yes, _____.

6. **Q:** You had a good time at the fashion show, _____?
   **A:** No, _____.

**B** | **Role-Playing.** Work with your partner. Pretend that one student is a famous fashion designer and the other student is a news reporter. The news reporter should ask the designer questions about the designer's company, style, favorite textiles, or recent projects. Use your imagination to come up with questions and answers. Be sure to use tag questions when asking your questions.

> You live and work in Paris, don't you?

> Yes, I do. I've lived there for 20 years now.

You are going to prepare and give a group presentation about fashion trends from a particular country.

**A** | **Discussion.** Form a group with two or three other students. Discuss the differences in fashion that you see in your city or area.

**B** | **Brainstorming.** Your group is going to brainstorm about fashion trends in a particular city, country, or area. As a group, decide on the location you want to talk about. If necessary, do additional research to find out more about the styles and fashions that are popular. Take notes in the chart below to help you organize your ideas.

A clothing store in Kabul, Afghanistan

A clothing market in Oruro, Bolivia

| What types of fabrics are popular? | |
| --- | --- |
| What clothing fashions are "in"? | |
| How do people wear their hair? | |
| What types of shoes do people prefer? | |
| What accessories do people like to wear? | |
| What other aspects of fashion are important? | |

**C** | **Planning a Presentation.** In your group, compare your notes from exercise **B**. Work together to plan and organize your presentation. (*See page 211 of the Independent Student Handbook for more information on planning and organizing your presentation.*)

**D** | **Presentation.** Give your presentation. Be sure that each group member gets a chance to speak during the presentation.

## Presentation Skills: Preparing Your Notes

Often you will use notes to help you remember what you want to say during a presentation. When you are preparing your notes, do not write out your presentation word-for-word. Instead, use key words, short sentences, or even pictures. Keep your notes organized and list points in the order you want to speak about them.

# Energy Issues

# Think and Discuss

1.  Look at the photo and read the caption. What types
    of energy are you familiar with?
2.  How much energy do you use in your daily life?

Vapor is released from a nuclear power plant in France.

# Exploring the Theme:
## Energy Issues

A | Look at the photos and read the captions. Then answer the questions.

1. How do you think energy use has changed over time?
2. In the future, do you think you will be using more or less electricity than you do now? Why do you think so?
3. Would you be willing to live next to a large energy facility such as a nuclear power plant or wind farm? Explain your answer.

Wind power provides energy to farms and homes in Abilene, Texas.

### Big Power, Big Risks

By the year 2030, the demand for energy is expected to be double what it was in the year 2000. Providing the enormous quantity of energy the world needs is a difficult task, and there is often risk for workers, the public, and the environment.

In this village, lights shine from nearly every house. However, the world is still far away from providing inexpensive electricity. In fact, about one in four people still have no electricity at all.

On April 20, 2010, one of the worst oil spills in history began in the Gulf of Mexico. The spill occurred at an oil rig, called the Deepwater Horizon, which is owned by the BP company. A buildup of pressure caused natural gas to shoot up suddenly from the ocean floor. The gas triggered a terrible explosion and a fire on the oil rig. After the explosion, the crew abandoned the platform and escaped in lifeboats. Unfortunately, eleven workers were never found.

A beach in the United States is covered with oil after the Deepwater Horizon oil spill.

For weeks, no one was sure just how much oil was being released into the Gulf of Mexico. Gradually, information about the damage from the oil spill emerged. It was discovered that between 50,000 to 60,000 barrels of oil a day were flowing into the Gulf. Experts from BP and other organizations tried to stop the spill, but it continued for nearly three months. By the time the leak was stopped, the beautiful blue waters of the Gulf had been contaminated with nearly 5 million barrels of oil.

Deepwater Horizon oil spill, Gulf of Mexico

The disaster did serious harm to the fishing and tourism industries in the southern United States. Pictures of birds that had been exposed to the thick oil appeared daily in the news. The American public reacted angrily, and the spill created a huge controversy. Some people even wanted to stop oil companies from drilling in the Gulf of Mexico. BP set aside 20 billion dollars to compensate fishermen, hotel owners, and store owners whose businesses were impacted by the spill.

**B** | Match each word in blue from exercise **A** with its definition. Use your dictionary to help you.

1. triggered (v.) _____
2. abandoned (v.) _____
3. released (v.) _____
4. emerged (v.) _____
5. experts (n.) _____
6. contaminated (v.) _____
7. exposed (v.) _____
8. reacted (v.) _____
9. controversy (n.) _____
10. compensate (v.) _____

a. to pay someone to replace lost money or things
b. became known; appeared
c. responded to
d. caused an event to begin to happen
e. left a place, thing, or person permanently
f. people who are very skilled or who know a lot about a particular subject
g. entered the surrounding atmosphere or area; freed
h. a disagreement, especially about a public policy or moral issue that people feel strongly about
i. made something dirty, harmful, or dangerous because of chemicals or radiation
j. placed in a dangerous situation

**A** | Read the interview and fill in each blank with the correct form of the word from the box. Use each word only once.

| abandon | controversy | expert | react | trigger |
|---------|-------------|--------|-------|---------|

**Q:** Can mining for energy sources such as coal and oil cause natural disasters?

**A:** Some people think so. For example, in 1989, there was an earthquake in the city of Newcastle, Australia. Some (1) _____ said it was (2) _____ by coal mining in the area. Others thought there was no way that mining 2297 feet (700 meters) down could cause an earthquake 6 miles (10 kilometers) beneath the surface of the earth.

**Q:** How did the public (3) _____ to the experts' opinion?

**A:** Well, it created a great deal of (4) _____. A lot of people called for an end to coal mining in Newcastle. John Tate, the Lord Mayor of the city at the time, said there was no chance Newcastle would (5) _____ coal mining.

Newcastle, Australia

 **B** | With a partner, practice the interview from exercise **A**. Then switch roles and practice again.

**C** | **Discussion.** Form a group with two or three other students and discuss the questions.

1. Eleven people died in the 1989 Newcastle earthquake. Should the coal-mining companies of Newcastle **compensate** the families of the workers who died? Explain your opinion.
2. What is your reaction when photos of an environmental disaster are **released**? Give an example.
3. The Deepwater Horizon oil spill **contaminated** the ocean and seashore. In your opinion, who is responsible for cleaning up the oil spill?
4. What could happen to animals, fish, and plants that are **exposed** to oil spills or dangerous gases from coal mines?
5. Following an environmental disaster, what do you think should happen if information **emerges** that shows the accident was caused by a company's or a government's negligence?[1]

[1]If someone is guilty of **negligence**, they have failed to do something that they ought to do.

# Before Listening

**Predicting Content.** Work with a partner. Look at the map and diagram. Discuss the questions.

1. Use your dictionary and look up these terms: *containment*, *radiation*, *radioactive*, *half-life*. How do you predict these words will be used in the lecture?
2. Locate the containment structure in the diagram. Why do you think this structure is important? Explain your ideas.

A modern nuclear power plant

## Listening: A Guest Speaker

### Critical Thinking Focus: Using an Outline to Take Notes

Using an outline can help you take organized and clear notes. In an outline, indicate main ideas with Roman numerals (I, II, III) and capital letters (A, B, C). Indicate details with numbers. As information becomes more specific, move it to the right.

track 2-3 **A** | Listen to the introduction to a lecture about the Chernobyl nuclear disaster. Read the outline as you listen.

I. Background
   A. 1970s & 1980s: Soviet Union developed nuclear technology
   B. 1986: 25 plants w/ safety probs.
II. Chernobyl disaster
   A. Causes
      1. Mistakes during safety test
      2. No containment building to limit fire and radiation
   B. Result: explosion→people dead

**B | Discussion.** With a partner, discuss the questions. Refer to the outline in exercise **A**.

1. What topics did the introduction cover?
2. Which items are main ideas? Which items are details?

**C | Listening for Main Ideas.** Listen to the entire lecture and answer the questions.

1. Check (✔) each effect of the explosion that the speaker mentions.
   ____ a. People were forced to leave their homes.
   ____ b. Animals died from exposure to radiation.
   ____ c. Young people became ill with thyroid cancer.
   ____ d. Billions of dollars were spent on health and cleanup costs.
   ____ e. Modern nuclear power plants are built with containment structures.
2. What happened to the town of Pripyat?
   a. It was abandoned.
   b. It burned to the ground.
   c. It was turned into a tourist attraction.
3. What is surprising about Chernobyl today?
   a. The residents of Pripyat have returned.
   b. Many animals have come back to the area.
   c. The radiation from the explosion has disappeared.

**D | Outlining.** Listen again. Continue the outline from exercise **A** on page 66. Complete the outline with details from the lecture. (*See page 206 of the Independent Student Handbook for more information on outlining.*)

C. The Chernobyl plant today
   1. Still extremely _____
   2. There are plans to build a _____
D. Radioactivity
   1. Many areas still contaminated with cesium _____
   2. Half-life of _____ years
E. The exclusion zone today
   1. _____ people live there
   2. Animals have returned, for ex., _____

## After Listening

**Discussion.** With a partner, answer the questions. Use your notes as well as your own ideas.

1. Describe the town of Pripyat before and after the disaster.
2. These days, a small number of tourists travel to Chernobyl. Would you go there if you had the opportunity?

# Language Function

 **A** | In the lecture about Chernobyl, the speaker used a number of useful expressions to emphasize her point. Listen to the excerpts and fill in the missing expressions.

track 2-5

1. _____ Chernobyl had no containment structure. This building would have limited the fire and contained the radioactivity.

2. Thyroid cancer can be cured, but _____ survivors must spend a lifetime taking medication.

3. _____, however, that it will be decades before large numbers of people are allowed to come back and live in the exclusion zone.

Wild horses, called Przewalski horses, walk through the Chernobyl exclusion zone. These horses are extinct in the wild and can only be found in a few nature reserves and in the Chernobyl exclusion zone.

**B** | Form a group with two other students. Choose one of the types of energy below and read the facts. Then tell the members of your group what you know about your energy source. Add your own ideas. Emphasize the fact that you think is the most interesting.

> Oil prices are rising. For example, it cost me almost $60 to put gas in my car yesterday. Last year, it would have cost me only $40. Still, it is important to remember that . . .

### Oil

- The price of oil is rising.
- Oil spills pollute the environment.
- The top three oil-producing countries in the world are Saudi Arabia, Russia, and the United States.

### Coal

- Coal deposits in the United States contain more energy than all the world's oil reserves combined.
- Coal is a relatively inexpensive energy source.
- Coal mining is dangerous. Between 1969 and 2000, more than 20,000 coal miners were killed.

### Wind

- Wind power is clean, but is sometimes very noisy.
- The world will never run out of wind.
- Denmark gets 20 percent of its electricity from wind power.

# Grammar

## The Future Perfect

The future perfect describes a state or a completed action in the future. We use this tense when the state or action will be completed by a specified future time or event. The future perfect is formed with *will + have +* the past participle.

> *If you start saving your money now, in ten years you **will have saved** enough money to retire.*

With the future perfect, a time expression is often used with *by* or *by the time.*

> ***By** my 30th birthday, I **will have graduated** from college.*

**A** | With a partner, complete these predictions about energy use in the future. Fill in each blank with the future perfect form of the verb in parentheses. Then take turns saying each sentence.

**2025** 1. By 2025, the capacity of batteries _____ (increase) by 1000 percent.

**2030** 2. By 2030, oil production _____ (return) to the level it was in 1980.

**2040** 3. By 2040, we will still be using oil, but its role _____ (change) significantly.

**2050** 4. By 2050, electric cars _____ completely _____ (replace) gasoline-powered cars.

**2060** 5. By 2060, corporations _____ (build) wind farms along the coasts of most nations.

**B** | **Self-Reflection.** Form a group with two or three other students. Use *by* or *by the time* and the future perfect to make predictions about your future. Respond to your classmates' sentences. Use the topics listed below to help your discussion.

- graduate from college
- get a job
- buy my first house
- buy a car
- learn to drive
- learn a new language

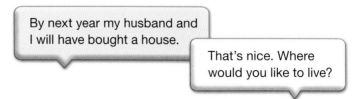

By next year my husband and I will have bought a house.

That's nice. Where would you like to live?

# Role-Playing a Town Meeting

 **A** | Form a group with three other students. You will role-play a city council meeting about building a nuclear power plant. Read the situation and the role cards. Assign two students to each role.

**Situation:** The city council has approved a plan to build a nuclear power plant in your city. A small group of residents are against the plan. They are going to meet with city council members to discuss their concerns.

### Role #1: Residents against the Nuclear Power Plant

1. Nuclear power plants aren't safe. We don't want a nuclear accident to happen here.

2. Nuclear power plants produce waste that is dangerous for many years.

3. People who live near a nuclear power plant might get cancer.

### Role #2: City Council Members

1. Nuclear safety technology has greatly advanced in recent years.

2. France, Belgium, and Slovakia rely on nuclear power for more than 50 percent of their electricity. There have been no big nuclear accidents in those countries.

3. Nuclear power could help us stop using oil.

 **B** | Work with the group member who shares your role. Think of more arguments to support your point. In addition, try to think of responses to the other side's arguments.

> I think they will say that . . .

> If they say that, we should emphasize that . . .

 **C** | **Role-Playing.** Role-play the discussion in your group. Use expressions of emphasis when appropriate.

> Thank you for meeting with us. We have a few concerns about this nuclear power plant.

> I understand. First of all, let me stress that we will do everything possible to make this power plant safe.

## Student to Student: Conceding a Point

In a debate or discussion, people often argue from different points of view. If an argument is very convincing to you, you can let the other person know that you agree with their point or that you accept that their point is true. Here are some expressions to concede a point.

*Good point.*
*Fair enough.*
*I'll give you that.*

Solar cells turn sunlight into electricity.

# SOLAR POWER

## Before Viewing

**Understanding Visuals.** Read the information. Use the words in blue to label the diagram.

There are many different kinds of solar power systems. This diagram shows how parabolic trough solar power works.

1. Sunlight hits curved mirrors that direct all the light and heat to the middle of the mirror.

2. In the middle of the mirror, a tube filled with synthetic[1] oil is heated to about 700°F.

3. The oil runs into a boiler where it turns water into steam.

4. The steam spins an electric turbine, which turns and makes electricity.

[1]**Synthetic** products are made from chemicals or artificial substances rather than from natural sources.

## While Viewing

**A** | Watch the video. Fill in the blanks with the word or words you hear.

The most powerful source of (1) _____ on the planet is actually out in space. It's (2) _____. More energy falls as sunlight on the United States in a single day than it uses in a (3) _____. But it's been difficult to turn that sunlight into (4) _____. Many people already use some (5) _____. But the world's need for power is great, and for solar power to be an alternative to other energy sources, it has to be both affordable and (6) _____.

**B** | Watch the video again. Check (✔) the five true statements.

1. ___ Sacramento doesn't use much solar power.
2. ___ Many new homes have solar cells.
3. ___ Many people drive solar-powered cars.
4. ___ Solar panels shade parking lots.
5. ___ Solar panels shade city buildings.
6. ___ Sacramento gets lower prices by buying a lot of solar panels at one time.
7. ___ Solar power is very expensive to residents of Sacramento.
8. ___ People can sell electricity back to the power company.

**C** | **Viewing for Specific Information.** Watch the video again. Circle the best answer to each question.

1. Where is the Kramer Solar Junction facility located?
   a. In the mountains
   b. In a desert
   c. By the sea
2. How many people can the facility provide power for?
   a. Half a million
   b. Five million
   c. Eight and a half million
3. What happens on days when there is no sun?
   a. The facility buys back power from customers.
   b. The facility uses power from batteries.
   c. The facility uses backup natural gas generators.
4. What does the facility produce a lot of?
   a. Power
   b. Carbon dioxide
   c. Smog

Ladybug robots crawl down a leaf. The robots are powered by solar power collectors attached to their backs.

## After Viewing

**Critical Thinking.** With a partner, discuss the questions.

1. What are some problems that could occur when using solar power?
2. In general, do you think the government should be responsible for developing alternative energies? Or, should it be left to private corporations to develop alternative energies? Explain your answer.
3. Mirrors now cover 1000 acres of the Mojave Desert at the Kramer Solar Junction power facility. What impact could this have on the local environment there?

track 2-6 **A** | **Meaning from Context.** Read and listen to the information. Notice the words in blue. These are words you will hear and use in Lesson B.

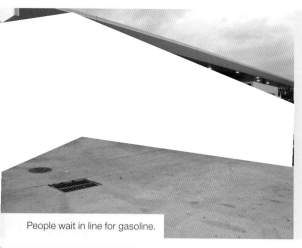

When oil was inexpensive and abundant, people learned to depend on it for heat and fuel. More recently, oil has been more difficult to find, as it is hidden deep beneath the earth under many layers of solid rock. There have even been oil shortages, and we have had to wait in long lines and pay high prices for gasoline. A serious disadvantage of oil, coal, and similar fuels is the pollution they create around our cities.

People wait in line for gasoline.

Today, researchers are focusing on energy sources beyond oil. Countries and companies are pursuing alternative energy. They are looking for energy sources that are renewable and can never be used up. These alternative energies follow the principle that energy production should be sustainable, not temporary. People are showing a lot of enthusiasm for new energy technologies such as wind and hydroelectric power. Government incentives in the form of money or tax breaks have helped convince some companies to develop alternative energy technologies. Experts think that in the future the world will utilize alternative energy for a larger percentage of its total energy needs.

Water is released at a hydroelectric dam.

**B** | Write each word in blue from exercise **A** next to its definition.

1. _____ (adj.) present or existing in large quantities
2. _____ (n.) the feeling of being very interested in or excited about something
3. _____ (n.) things that encourage you to want to work hard or take action
4. _____ (n.) pieces of a material or substance that cover a surface or are between two other things
5. _____ (v.) making an effort to achieve a goal
6. _____ (n.) a factor which makes a person or a thing less useful or successful than other people or things
7. _____ (n.) a general belief about the way something should behave
8. _____ (v.) to use
9. _____ (adj.) resources that are natural and always available, such as wind and sunlight
10. _____ (n.) conditions in which there is not enough of something

**A** | What do you know about geothermal energy? Work with a partner and take the quiz. Circle **T** for *true* and **F** for *false*. Then check your answers at the bottom of the page. Which of these facts surprised you? Explain.

**GEOTHERMAL ENERGY: What do you know?**

1. Geothermal energy is a type of renewable energy. **T  F**

2. Geothermal energy is found in the layers of rock beneath the earth's surface. **T  F**

3. Geothermal energy is the most abundant energy source on earth. **T  F**

4. The U.S. government offers incentives to homeowners to install geothermal systems in their homes. **T  F**

5. Geothermal energy works on the same principle as the steam engine: when water is converted to steam, it produces force. **T  F**

6. Geothermal energy has been utilized for cooking and heating only in the past 50 years. **T  F**

Visitors swim in a hot spring created by geothermal energy. Geothermal energy is derived from the earth's internal heat.

**B** | **Self-Reflection.** With your partner, discuss the questions.

1. Do you plan to pursue more education sometime in the future? Explain.
2. What is a hobby or activity that you are enthusiastic about? Why do you enjoy it?
3. There is a shortage of nurses in the world. Would you ever consider becoming a nurse? Explain.
4. Do you have an incentive for learning English? What is it?
5. Do you think that people who avoid technology are at a disadvantage compared to people who use technology often? Explain.

**ANSWERS: The false statements are #3 (Other sources such as coal are more abundant.); #4 (The government offers incentives to install solar systems, but not geothermal.); and #6 (Geothermal energy has been used for thousands of years.)**

# Before Listening

**👥 Understanding Visuals.** Work with a partner. Look at the diagrams. How do wind and hydroelectric systems generate electricity? Share some ideas with your partner. (*See page 216 of the Independent Student Handbook for more information on understanding visuals.*)

# Listening: A Study Group Discussion

**🎧 track 2-7 A | Listening for Key Concepts.** Listen to a student speaking at the beginning of a study group meeting. Are these statements true or false? Circle **T** for *true* or **F** for *false*.

| | | | |
|---|---|---|---|
| 1. | The group is meeting for the first time. | **T** | **F** |
| 2. | The group is preparing for a presentation. | **T** | **F** |
| 3. | The presentation is about renewable energies. | **T** | **F** |
| 4. | The first speaker will talk about fossil fuels. | **T** | **F** |
| 5. | The next speaker will talk about wind energy. | **T** | **F** |

**🎧 track 2-8 B | Using a Graphic Organizer.** Listen to students presenting their research on solar, wind, and hydroelectric power. Complete the notes in the T-charts below and on page 77.

| Solar Power Advantages | Solar Power Disadvantages |
|---|---|
| 1. No fire = no _____ | 1. Cost of _____ |
| 2. Free | 2. _____ cut off energy supply |
| 3. 100% _____ | 3. _____ technology isn't good enough yet |

| Wind Power Advantages | Wind Power Disadvantages |
|---|---|
| 1. Clean, renewable | 1. Look _____ |
| 2. No emissions = no _____ | 2. Turbines make _____ |
| 3. Costs _____ | 3. No wind = no _____ |
| 4. Many govs. offer _____ | 4. Tech. for _____ hasn't been developed yet |

| Hydroelectric Power Advantages | Hydroelectric Power Disadvantages |
|---|---|
| 1. Water is _____ | 1. Damage to _____ |
| 2. Once built, doesn't need _____ | 2. Destroys _____ |
| 3. No _____ | 3. Forces people _____ |
| 4. Cost: _____ | |

# After Listening

**Critical Thinking.** Using your notes from pages 76 and 77, discuss the questions with a partner.

1. Which advantages do all three forms of energy share?
2. Imagine that your community has decided to build a renewable energy facility. Which energy source is best for your area? Consider the advantages and disadvantages of solar, wind, and hydroelectric power. Also consider the environment and weather in your area.

# Pronunciation

**Stressing Two-Word Compounds**

track 2-9

In many two-word compounds, the stress is on the first word.

**book** review      **foot**print      **green**house      **living** room      **moving** van

Stressing both words in these situations can sound strange or can change the meaning of the sentence.

*The peas were grown in a **green**house.* (a glass building for growing plants)
*I saw you standing in front of a **green house**.* (a house painted the color green)

track 2-10

**A** | Listen to each sentence and check (✔) the correct meaning of the underlined phrase.

1. I met an English teacher.
   ❏ a teacher of the English language          ❏ a teacher who is English
2. I had a glass of orange juice.
   ❏ juice made from oranges          ❏ orange-colored juice, maybe mango
3. The police spotted a moving van.
   ❏ a van in motion          ❏ a large van for moving furniture
4. Where should I put this hot plate?
   ❏ a plate that is hot          ❏ a small stove for keeping food warm
5. That's a beautiful yellow jacket.
   ❏ a flying insect          ❏ a coat

**B** | With a partner, take turns saying the sentences from exercise **A**. Stress either the first underlined word or both of the underlined words. Your partner will tell you the meaning of the word or phrase he or she hears.

# Language Function

track 2-11

**A** | In the study group discussion, there were a number of expressions for expressing approval and disapproval. Listen and fill in the missing expressions you hear.

1. On the downside, some people _____ wind turbines because they're ugly. They also complain about the noise the machines make, although most people think _____ put up wind turbines on farmlands.

2. A lot of people think _____ to destroy animal habitats this way. They also believe _____ that people are forced to leave their homes.

**B** | Read the statements. Use the ratings below to indicate your approval or disapproval of each topic.

1 = strongly approve   2 = approve   3 = neither approve nor disapprove   4 = disapprove   5 = strongly disapprove

| Statements | My Rating |
|---|---|
| a. The city council has voted to raise taxes by one percent in order to put solar energy systems in all government buildings. Do you approve or disapprove of raising taxes? | |
| b. A dam will provide cheap hydroelectric power to millions of people. However, it will require hundreds of people to leave the valley where they have been living for many years. Do you approve or disapprove of building the dam? | |
| c. A proposed geothermal plant near your town will reduce your energy bills. However, the steam that is released contains a gas that smells like rotten eggs. Do you approve or disapprove of building the geothermal plant? | |
| d. Your neighbor wants to install a wind turbine in his backyard. Do you approve or disapprove? | |

**C** | **Discussion.** Form a group with three other students and compare your ratings from exercise **B**. One student should read each statement. Then group members should take turns giving and explaining their ratings. Discuss whether you agree or disagree with your classmates' ratings.

# Grammar

**The Future Perfect Progressive**

The future perfect progressive is used to talk about actions that will be in progress before a specific time in the future. This tense is formed with *will* + *have* + *been* + the present participle.

> By 2020, we **will have been drilling** oil wells for over 160 years.

The future perfect progressive emphasizes the duration of an action up to a specific future time. Often, this tense is used with a time expression and *for*.

> In just two weeks, we will have been meeting **for three months**.

**A** | Complete the sentences with the future perfect progressive form of the verb in parentheses.

1. In June of next year, my father _____ (living) in Brazil for 10 years.

2. In November, that company _____ (sell) wind turbines for six months.

3. On his next birthday, John _____ (drive) for 15 years.

4. In 2025, France _____ (produce) electricity with nuclear power for 60 years.

5. Next February, Sally _____ (work) as a nurse for 25 years.

6. In 2030, Iceland _____ (use) geothermal energy to heat homes for 100 years.

7. By next year, my book club _____ (meeting) for 5 years.

**B** | Fill in the blanks with the future perfect or the future perfect progressive form of the verb in parentheses.

I've been thinking about going to college for a while. In fact, by the end of June I (1) _____ (work) for two years. At that point, I'd like to quit my job and start studying. I have decided to get a degree in business at City University. By January 30, I (2) _____ (submit) my application. I hope that by May I (3) _____ (received) their answer. I hope to study with Professor Morse. He is very experienced. By next year, he (4) _____ (teach) business courses for more than 20 years. The local government wants people to study, so they began giving financial incentives to students last year. By the time I graduate, they (5) _____ (give) financial incentives for five years.

**C** | **Discussion.** With a partner, discuss the questions.

Which of these inventions and technologies do you use? When did you start using them? By 2025, how long will you have been using them? Talk about additional technologies that you use often.

- video games
- smart phone
- personal computer
- high-definition television

> I started using a cell phone in 2003. By 2025, I will have been using a cell phone for 22 years!

Your group is going to deliver a presentation to the class about an unusual source of energy. To support your presentation, your group will make a poster or a slide presentation with pictures, graphs, or other visual information. Your visual should include answers to these questions:

1. What is an unusual source of energy?
2. How does this energy source work?
3. What are the advantages and disadvantages of using this energy source?

**A** | **Discussion.** Form a group of two or three students. Examine the list of unusual energy sources and select one to research.

This biomass plant burns rice to generate electricity.

biodiesel                        hydrogen fuel cells
biomass                          methane from landfills
energy-generating floors         sugar
ethanol                          tidal or ocean power

**B** | **Researching.** Outside of class, research your topic online or in the library. Use the outline below as a guide while you take notes about your topic. Find several images that relate to your energy source. (*See page 212 of the Independent Student Handbook for more information on doing research.*)

I. Type of energy
   A. Description
   B. Source
II. Examples of how the energy is used
   A. Places
   B. Purposes
III. Advantages
IV. Disadvantages
V. Future of this form of energy

**C** | **Planning a Presentation.** As a group, use your notes from exercise **B** and your images to create a poster or slide presentation about your energy source. Be sure that your poster or slide presentation answers the three questions in the box at the top of the page.

**D** | **Presentation.** When you give your presentation, all group members should speak. Be sure to explain the images you present, and answer any questions from your audience.

## Presentation Skills: Fighting Nervousness

It is normal to be a little nervous at the beginning of a presentation. However, the first impression you make on your audience is very important. Make an effort to speak slowly and calmly at the beginning of your presentation. Memorizing the first few sentences you plan to say can sometimes help. Soon you will begin to feel more comfortable and gain confidence.

# Migration

ACADEMIC PATHWAYS
Lesson A:  Listening to a Radio Show
          Talking about Your Family History
Lesson B:  Listening to a Conversation between Friends
           Doing a Research-Based Presentation

## Think and Discuss

1. Look at the photo. Where do you think these birds are going?
2. What are some of the reasons that people and animals move in large numbers?
3. Where on our planet do you believe the first human beings lived? Why do you think so?

Migrating snow geese and Canada geese fly as the sun sets.

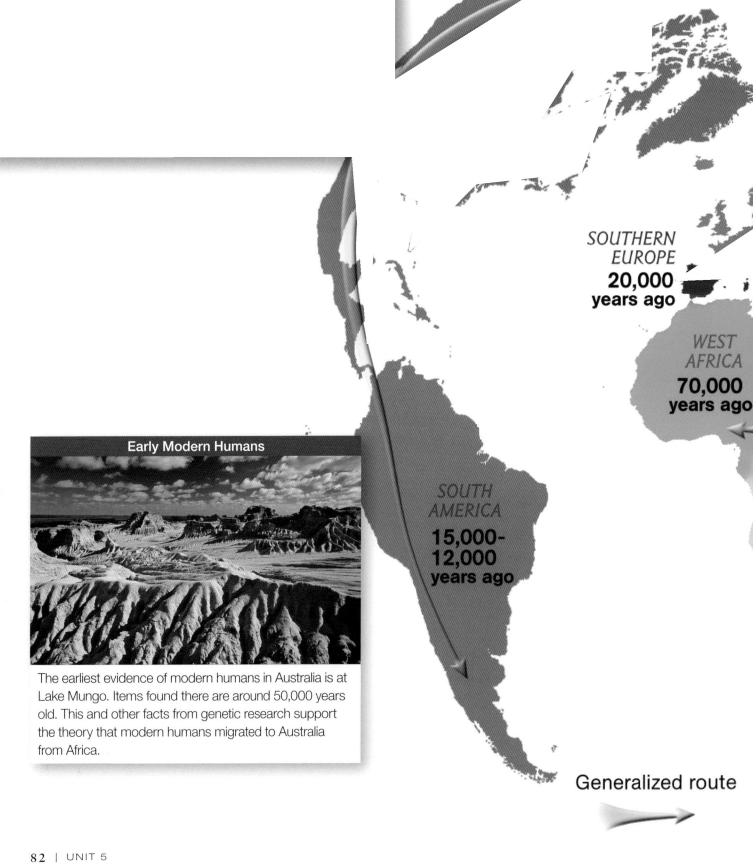

**SOUTHERN
EUROPE
20,000
years ago**

**WEST
AFRICA
70,000
years ago**

**SOUTH
AMERICA
15,000–
12,000
years ago**

**Early Modern Humans**

The earliest evidence of modern humans in Australia is at Lake Mungo. Items found there are around 50,000 years old. This and other facts from genetic research support the theory that modern humans migrated to Australia from Africa.

Generalized route

**Neanderthals**

When early modern humans migrated to Europe, they met the Neanderthals. Evidence shows that the Neanderthals were squeezed into smaller and smaller areas and disappeared.

SIBERIA
**30,000 years ago**

EAST ASIA
**30,000 years ago**

CENTRAL ASIA

SOUTHEAST ASIA
**50,000 years ago**

**50,000 years ago**

MIDDLE EAST

SOUTH ASIA

EAST RICA

**200,000 years ago**

AUSTRALIA
**50,000 years ago**

**The Human Journey**

Humans all over the world migrate to new locations in search of food, water, and living space. This map shows how early modern humans spread throughout the world.

Migration date
**30,000 years ago**

**A | Meaning from Context.** Read and listen to the information about migration. Notice the words in **blue**. These are words you will hear and use in Lesson A.

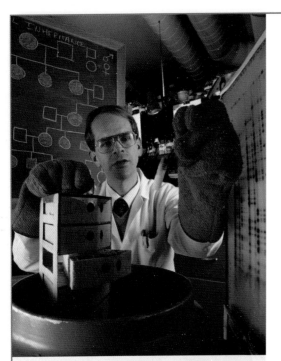
A scientist studies DNA and other genetic material.

The first **migrations** in human history were probably voluntary. People chose to leave their birthplace in search of food, water, or living space. Other migrations have been involuntary, which means that people were forced to travel. Between the 16th and 19th centuries, for instance, European slave traders kidnapped an **immense** number of African natives and transported them against their will to the Americas. There, the Africans **encountered** a world unlike anything they had ever seen in their native lands. They were forced to work in terrible conditions, and many died young.

The practice of slavery **declined** in the 18th and 19th centuries. **Subsequently**, it was made illegal, and the descendants[1] of those early African slaves became free. Africans were **absorbed** into the cultures of the Americas, and today they are described, for example, as African Americans, Afro-Caribbeans, or Afro-Latin Americans.

In recent years, DNA[2] researchers believe that they have **linked** the DNA of all humans on our planet with the DNA of African natives. Scientists **assume** that the entire world was populated as a result of a migration that began in Africa around 70,000 years ago. The **implications** of this idea would have shocked the European slave traders. They probably would have found it **incredible** to think that people all over the world were, in a sense, related to one another.

[1]Someone's **descendants** are the people in later generations who are related to them.
[2]**DNA** is a substance that carries information in the cells of the body. It is responsible for characteristics being passed on from parents to their children.

**B |** Write each word in **blue** from exercise **A** next to its definition.

1. _____ (n.) unstated conclusions based on given facts
2. _____ (adv.) later or afterwards
3. _____ (adj.) very unusual, surprising, or difficult to believe
4. _____ (v.) met someone unexpectedly
5. _____ (n.) large-scale movements of people or animals
6. _____ (adj.) extremely large or great amounts
7. _____ (v.) became less in quantity, importance, or strength
8. _____ (v.) take something into a larger group and make it part of the group
9. _____ (v.) connected physically or logically
10. _____ (v.) to believe something to be true, although it is not a proven fact

**A | Using a Dictionary.** Complete the paragraph with the correct form of a word from the box. Use your dictionary to help you.

absorb          assume          implication          migrate          subsequently

Early modern humans (1) _____ to Britain around 30,000 years ago. (2) _____, however, most left just 3000 years later. Britain became very cold when an ice age began, and early modern humans left to find warmer areas. Humans returned to Britain when temperatures became warm again. Until recently, scientists (3) _____ that people returned slowly and in small numbers. Now, however, scientists believe that humans actually returned very quickly and in large numbers. Scientists developed this theory by using *carbon dating*. Carbon dating is a process used to tell exactly how old an object is by measuring the amount of

Early modern humans hunt during the ice age.

carbon-14 it contains. Carbon-14 is a natural material that living things (4) _____ until they die. In Britain, scientists discovered the bones of a large number of animals such as horses and hares. The bones had marks on them showing that the animals had been killed and cut up by humans with tools. Scientists used carbon dating and found that the animals were killed very soon after the ice age ended. The (5) _____ was clear to the scientists: A large number of humans had followed the animals back to Britain soon after the temperature warmed.

**B | Discussion.** With a partner, answer the questions.

1. Early humans traveled **immense** distances to populate the world. Tell your partner about the longest trip you have ever taken.
2. Choose a time or a place in human history that you find **incredible**. Explain to your partner why you find this event interesting.
3. When old cultures **encounter** newer ones, both cultures change in positive and negative ways. What types of changes could happen when two cultures meet? Share your ideas with your partner.
4. In many developed countries, such as Italy and Japan, the population is **declining**. What effects might this have on these countries?

**C | Choosing the Right Definition.** Study the numbered definitions for link. Write the number of the definition next to the correct sentence below.

_____ a. Thousands of years ago there was a link between Asia and North America.

_____ b. Her necklace fell to the floor when one of the links broke.

_____ c. There is a link between exercise and good health.

**link** /lɪŋk/ **(links, linking, linked)**
[1] N-COUNT If there is a **link** between two things, there is a relationship between them; for example, one thing causes or affects the other. • *the link between cell phones and car accidents*   [2] N-COUNT A **link** between two things or places is a physical connection between them. • *A tunnel links between England and France.*   [3] N-COUNT A **link** is one of the rings in a chain. • *a broken link on a bicycle chain*

# Before Listening

👥 **Predicting Content.** With a partner, discuss the questions.

1. Look at the photos. Can you guess which of these people are related to each other? After you have guessed, look at the answer at the bottom of the page.

2. Sometimes, people who are genetically related look very different from one another. How does this happen?
3. Do you and your relatives look alike, or are there members of your family who look very different from everyone else? Explain.

# Listening: A Radio Show

### Critical Thinking Focus: Understanding Scientific Theories

In science, a *theory* is a general principle that is used to explain or predict events. Scientists look for *evidence* to prove that a theory is correct. For example, the evidence from carbon-14 dating supports the theory that humans returned to Britain shortly after the end of the ice age.

track 2-13

**A | Listening for Key Concepts.** Listen to the radio show and choose the best answer to each question. (*See page 202 of the Independent Student Handbook for more information on improving listening skills.*)

1. Which of these would be a good title for the radio show?
   a. Modern Humans—Not Neanderthal Descendants
   b. New Research Links Modern Humans to Africa
   c. Modern Humans Settled South America Last

2. What type of evidence does Dr. Corke mainly rely on?
   a. DNA research
   b. Ancient bones and tools
   c. Animal migration paths

3. Which statement about Neanderthals is true?
   a. They became modern humans.
   b. They crossed into the Americas.
   c. They no longer exist.

**ANSWER:** All of the people in the photos are related either closely or distantly to the woman on the far left.

**B** | **Note-Taking.** Listen again. As you listen, complete the timeline about human migration. (*See page 206 of the Independent Student Handbook for more information on note-taking.*)

| **150,000 years ago** | **50–70,000 years ago** | **30,000 years ago** | **20,000 years ago** |
|---|---|---|---|
| Ancestors of all people alive today lived in Africa | Group of ppl. left _____ & arrived in _____ | 2 grps. reached _____ & _____ | _____ _____ |

**C** | **Listening for Details.** Listen again. Match each sentence beginning with the correct ending.

_____ 1. The group that followed the coast around the Arabian Peninsula and India . . .

_____ 2. The group that moved into Europe . . .

_____ 3. The group that migrated into Central Asia . . .

_____ 4. People who lived in southern Siberia . . .

a. probably encountered fewer Neanderthals.

b. eventually reached Australia if the DNA evidence is correct.

c. most likely migrated to North America between 15,000 and 20,000 years ago.

d. probably encountered a larger number of Neanderthals.

## After Listening

**Critical Thinking.** Form a group with two or three other students. Discuss the questions.

1. According to the information in the radio show, what could cause people with the same genetic ancestor to look very different from one another?
2. Dr. Corke said that "there is no evidence of Neanderthal DNA in the DNA of modern humans." What does this imply about the relationship between modern humans and Neanderthals?
3. In what ways do you think humans have changed over time?

# Language Function

 **A** | Read the information about expressing surprise. Then listen and repeat the expressions in the box.

 **B** | In the radio show, the speakers used a number of useful phrases for expressing surprise. Listen and fill in the missing expressions.

1. **Dr. Corke:** This difference, called a mutation, is then passed down to all of that person's descendants, even 50,000 years in the future.

   **Interviewer:** _____!

2. **Dr. Corke:** If they're right, all people are linked to that woman through their mothers.

   **Interviewer:** _____.

3. **Dr. Corke:** We don't think they were absorbed into the modern human family. If they had been absorbed, DNA analysis would tell us that, you see. The evidence would be there in the DNA of Europeans today.

   **Interviewer:** _____! DNA certainly does tell us a lot!

**C** | Take turns telling a partner information about yourself. React to your partner's information, and use an expression of surprise if you are truly surprised.

> I have lived in 13 different countries in my life.

> That's incredible! What countries did you live in?

**D | Discussion.** Work with your partner. One student is Student A and the other is Student B. Read the animal facts to your partner. Respond to your partner with an expression of surprise from the box. Discuss any facts that are very surprising to you.

> Giraffes and humans have the same number of bones in their neck—seven.

> That's really surprising. I thought giraffes would have a lot more bones than humans have.

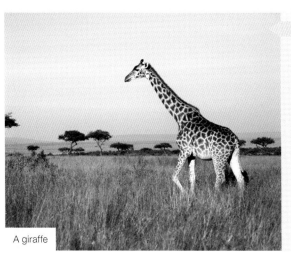
A giraffe

### Student A

1. Giraffes and humans have the same number of bones in their necks—seven.
2. Cows cause more human deaths each year than sharks do.
3. Cockroaches can live as long as nine days without their heads, because the brain of the insect is located in its body.
4. It is estimated that there are nearly two billion cats in the world today.
5. The blue whale weighs 170 tons, which is about as much as 22 elephants.

A murder of crows

### Student B

1. Any group of birds can be called a flock, but a group of crows is also called a murder of crows.
2. Deer are responsible for more human injuries and deaths than any other animal due to the many traffic accidents they cause.
3. Scientists have identified about 1.7 million species of animals, but there are many more species that have not been identified yet. There could be more unidentified species than identified ones.
4. The skin of a polar bear is actually black. Black skin helps the bears absorb as much of the sun's heat as possible.
5. Whiskers allow a cat to judge the width of a space, and whether it can fit into the space or not.

# Grammar

## Using Past Modals to Make Guesses about the Past

To make guesses about the past, use *could have*, *may have*, or *might have* and a past participle.

> Modern humans entering Central Asia **could have run** into Neanderthals.

In short responses that are guesses, do not use the past participle.

> A: Did they come from Siberia?
> B: They **may have**.

When the verb *be* is used, keep the past participle in the sentence.

> A: Were there 1000 people in the group?
> B: There **might have been**.

**A** | Form a group with two or three other students. Read the situations and make guesses about what happened for each situation. Use *could have*, *may have*, *might have,* and the past participle of a verb.

1. Samantha walked halfway to the bus stop this morning, then suddenly turned around and walked back to her house. Why did she turn around?

> She could have left the stove on.
>
> She may have left her wallet at home.
>
> She might have forgotten to lock the door.

2. Yesterday, Ali had to go to the hospital after playing basketball. What was wrong with him?
3. Dana got more exercise today than she has in years. What did she do?
4. In the 20th century, millions of people migrated to the United States. Why did they leave their own countries to go there?

**B** | **Discussion.** With a partner, discuss these questions about the early modern humans who left Africa. Make guesses using *could have*, *may have*, and *might have*. Give reasons for your guesses.

1. What did the early modern humans eat? How did they hunt?
2. What did they wear?
3. What were their families like?
4. What kinds of homes did they live in?
5. What tools did they use?
6. How did they spend their free time?

> They might have eaten vegetables that they planted.
>
> I don't know about that. You need to stay in one place to farm vegetables. These people may have moved around too much.

# Talking about Your Family History

**A** | **Using a Graphic Organizer.** Where did your family members come from originally? If they left that place, where did they go? Fill in the chart with information about your family. If you are not sure about something, write a question mark. (*See page 214 of the Independent Student Handbook for more information on using graphic organizers.*)

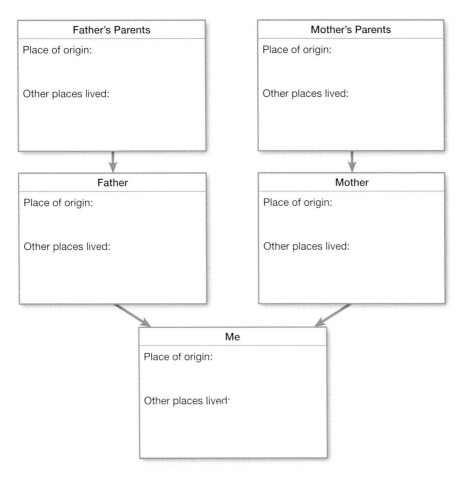

| Father's Parents | Mother's Parents |
|---|---|
| Place of origin: | Place of origin: |
| Other places lived: | Other places lived: |

| Father | Mother |
|---|---|
| Place of origin: | Place of origin: |
| Other places lived: | Other places lived: |

| Me |
|---|
| Place of origin: |
| Other places lived: |

**B** | **Discussion.** Form a group with two or three other students. Use the information from exercise **A** to talk about migration in your family. State the people's place of origin and other places where they lived. If you are not sure about where a family member came from, use *could have*, *may have*, or *might have* and make a guess. React to other members of your group and use expressions of surprise where appropriate.

> I was born in Chicago and my parents were born in Holland. They came to the United States in 1967. I'm not sure about my mother's parents. I think they may have migrated from Poland.

> No kidding! That's where my grandmother is from.

**Student to Student:**
**Expressing Interest**

Use these expressions when another person is talking to show you are interested in what they are saying:

*That's (really) interesting.*
*How interesting/fascinating.*
*Really?*
*How about that!*

Migrating wildebeest cross a river.

The Serengeti

## Before Viewing

**A** | **Understanding Visuals.** You are going to watch a video about a yearly migration of wildebeest. Look at the map on this page and answer the questions.

1. Which two countries does the wildebeest migration travel through?

   _____

   _____

2. Use the map key to follow the migration of the wildebeest throughout the year. Where are the wildebeest today?

**B** | **Using a Dictionary.** You will hear these words in the video. Match each word with its definition. Use your dictionary to help you.

1. calf (n.)       ____
2. carcass (n.)   ____
3. graze (v.)      ____
4. herd (n.)       ____
5. predator (n.)  ____

a. to eat grass or other growing plants
b. a large group of animals of one kind
c. an animal that kills and eats other animals
d. a young wildebeest
e. the body of a dead animal

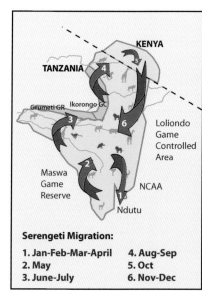

**Serengeti Migration:**

1. Jan-Feb-Mar-April   4. Aug-Sep
2. May                 5. Oct
3. June-July           6. Nov-Dec

Millions of animals such as wildebeest and zebras migrate through the Serengeti National Park, shown here in green.

## While Viewing

**A | Sequencing Events.** Watch the video. Number the events in order from 1 to 5. The first event has already been numbered for you.

_____ a. The wildebeest graze in the Masai Mara.

__1__ b. The wildebeest give birth.

_____ c. The wildebeest arrive at the Masai Mara.

_____ d. The migration begins.

_____ e. The wildebeest arrive back at the Serengeti.

**B | Note-Taking.** Watch the video again. Complete the student notes with information from the video.

An elephant crosses the road in the Serengeti National Park.

## Wildebeest Migration

- 2 mil. animals travel _____ miles
- At beginning of yr., all wildebeest give _____ in same month
  - Calves can run _____ 2 days after birth
- Nobody knows what triggers _____
- 200,000 of the _____ wildebeest will die from starvation, disease, and overexertion
  - Others die from predators; cat tries to separate calf from _____
- Kenya's Masai Mara: _____ create huge area of _____
- In _____ , the wildebeest head south again to the _____ .

## After Viewing

**Critical Thinking.** Discuss the questions with a partner.

1. In the video, you heard that "no one knows what triggers the migration." What are some possible explanations for why the wildebeest start their migration?
2. Recently, the government of Tanzania wanted to build a highway across the Serengeti National Park. The road would have cut across the migration routes of the wildebeest. What arguments could be made against building this highway? What arguments could be made in favor of building it?

**A** | **Meaning from Context.** Read and listen to the interview about butterfly migration. Notice the words in blue. These are words you will hear and use in Lesson B.

| | |
|---|---|
| **Interviewer:** | I'm talking with Maxine Felton, a butterfly expert. For more than 20 years she has dedicated herself to the study of butterflies. What kinds of butterflies do you study, Maxine? |
| **Maxine:** | I study the monarch butterfly. It is an orange, black, and white butterfly that's approximately 10 centimeters across. |
| **Interviewer:** | What is special about the monarch butterfly? |
| **Maxine:** | Well, it is the only butterfly that migrates north to south with the seasons, the same way that many birds do. |

A woman takes a photo of hundreds of butterflies.

| | |
|---|---|
| **Interviewer:** | How interesting! And how do you follow the monarch butterfly migration? |
| **Maxine:** | Well, I glue little numbered labels on their wings. The labels help me follow their migration patterns. The labels are small, so they don't interfere with flying. Nighttime is the best time to glue on the labels, because monarchs stay on the ground at night. Their flying is restricted to the daylight hours. |
| **Interviewer:** | And where do the monarchs go in the winter? |
| **Maxine:** | Many go to the Mexican Monarch Butterfly Reserve. When the butterflies arrive there, they cover the trees in overwhelming numbers. |
| **Interviewer:** | That must be a beautiful sight! It sounds like there are plenty of monarchs. |
| **Maxine:** | Well, actually, there are fewer than there once were. There are various threats to monarchs. For example, in the Butterfly Reserve some illegal logging still takes place. In many places, plants such as corn and wheat have displaced many of the milkweed plants that monarchs need for food. |
| **Interviewer:** | I see. Is there any good news for monarch butterflies? |
| **Maxine:** | Yes, there is. Many new conservation agencies and areas have been established to protect monarchs. Recently, the World Wildlife Fund, the Mexican government, and Mexican billionaire Carlos Slim invested 100 million dollars in a fund to protect wildlife in Mexico. Part of the money will help to ensure the continued protection of monarch butterflies in Mexico. |

 **B** | **Self-Reflection.** With a partner, discuss the questions below.

1. If you had 100 million dollars to invest, what would you spend it on? Explain your choices.
2. Do you think it is OK for scientists to track animals as long as their efforts don't interfere with the animals' migration? Why, or why not?

**A** | Complete the paragraph with the correct form of a word from the box.

approximately          ensure          illegal          invest
displace               establish        interfere        overwhelming

Salmon fishing in the Pacific Ocean is a huge business. In a good year, (1) _____ 800,000 tons of salmon are caught, but today salmon populations are facing (2) _____ challenges. River dams are one problem. Salmon are migrating fish that must return far up rivers and streams to the spot where they were born in order to reproduce.[1] Dams built on rivers can (3) _____ with salmon

Salmon swim upstream.

migration and, as a result, with salmon reproduction. Drift nets in the ocean are another obstacle. These nets, which are 32 feet (10 meters) across and 30 miles (48 kilometers) long, are (4) _____ in many countries because they kill too much sea life. Still, certain countries continue to use them.

As competition for wild salmon increases, new ways of meeting the demand are being tested. Farmers have (5) _____ salmon farms where the fish are raised in saltwater cages. The farms have been very successful, and farm-raised salmon has (6) _____ wild salmon in many restaurants. Moreover, some countries have (7) _____ money to help raise and release young salmon in rivers and streams. These salmon make their way to the ocean, where they grow to adulthood. Many will be caught and eaten, but the ones that return upstream will produce millions of babies to (8) _____ that salmon will survive.

[1]When people, animals, or plants **reproduce**, they produce babies.

 **B** | **Critical Thinking.** Work with a partner. Read the information and discuss the questions.

Salmon travel through the national waters of many countries without restrictions. The governments of the United States and Canada believe that every migrating salmon belongs to the country where it was born, no matter where it goes in the ocean. The fishermen of some countries believe that fish, a gift of nature, belong to everyone. These fishermen believe that they should be able to catch and keep the salmon.

1. Which position do you agree with? Explain your reasons.
2. If a fisherman catches a migrating salmon, how could he figure out if it is a migrating salmon from a different country?

# Before Listening

👥👥 **Prior Knowledge.** Form a group with two or three other students. Look at the photos and read the captions. Then discuss the questions.

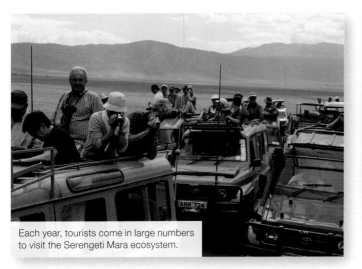

Each year, tourists come in large numbers to visit the Serengeti Mara ecosystem.

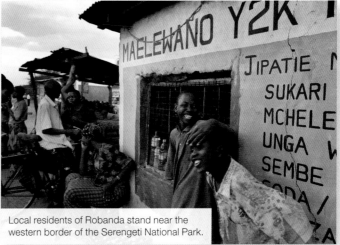

Local residents of Robanda stand near the western border of the Serengeti National Park.

1. Where were these photos taken? Do you know anyone who has been to this place?
2. Why have tourists with cameras come to this place?
3. Do you think tourism helps or hurts the people of Robanda? Explain.

## Listening: A Conversation between Friends

🎧 track 2-17 **A** | **Listening for Main Ideas.** Listen to Sandy and Larry talking about Larry's trip. Circle the correct answers.

1. The size of the Serengeti Mara ecosystem has _____.
   a. increased          b. decreased

2. The human populations in Kenya and Tanzania have been _____.
   a. increasing          b. decreasing

3. The Robandans _____ to accept money to move from their village.
   a. want          b. don't want

4. Animal populations in the Serengeti Mara ecosystem are _____.
   a. in trouble          b. doing all right

🎧 track 2-17 **B** | Read the statements. Then listen again. Circle **T** for *true* or **F** for *false*.

1. Sandy has been to Tanzania to see the wildebeest migration before.          **T**          **F**
2. Bush meat is an important source of food in northern Tanzania.          **T**          **F**
3. Wildebeest are the only animals in the Serengeti Mara ecosystem.          **T**          **F**
4. The Ikoma people did not want to leave the park in 1951.          **T**          **F**
5. The people of Robanda have agreed to accept money to move again.          **T**          **F**

# After Listening

**Critical Thinking.** Discuss the questions with a partner.

1. In your own words, explain the conflict between the needs of the animals and the needs of people of the Serengeti Mara ecosystem.
2. If you were villagers from Robanda, would you accept the offer of money to move off the land? Why, or why not?
3. In Tanzania, successful ecotourism corporations can be extremely powerful. How can the government of Tanzania make sure that corporations do not abuse their power?

# Pronunciation

## Using Question Intonation

In most *yes/no* questions, the intonation rises at the last content word in the sentence. Content words are words that are important to the meaning of the sentence.

track 2-18

*Do you have the time?*

*Can you show me the pictures you took?*

In *wh-* questions, the intonation rises and then falls at the end of the sentence.

*How was your trip?*          *When did you get there?*

track 2-19

**A** | Listen to the questions. Draw intonation lines like the ones in the box above.

1. Have you ever tried bush meat? Would you like to?

2. Why do animals migrate? What about humans?

3. Is migrating dangerous for animals? What are the risks?

4. How many tourists visit Tanzania each year?

5. Do you enjoy photography?

6. Should the people of Robanda be forced to move?

**B** | With a partner, take turns asking and answering the questions from exercise **A**. Be sure to use correct question intonation.

## Expressing Hopes

We use the following expressions to express hopes about the future.

*I (really) hope (that) . . .*
*I'm hoping (that)  . . .*
*It would be nice/great/wonderful/ideal if . . .*

track 2-20

**A** | In the conversation, Larry and Sandy used a number of useful expressions for expressing hopes. Listen and fill in the missing expressions.

1. **Larry:** _____ there were enough land for people and for animals, but there isn't.

2. **Sandy:** Hmm. _____ that some compromise can be reached.

3. **Sandy:** What a wonderful trip you had! I'm really jealous! _____ to go on a trip like that.

**B** | **Role-Playing.** Form a group with two or three other students. As a group, choose one of the following scenarios and role-play the situation. Be sure to use phrases for expressing hopes.

1. Your city council has announced plans to build a new community center. Talk about your hopes for the new community center. For example, you can talk about the location, the cost, and the activities and classes that you want the community center to have.

> I hope that the community center isn't too far away.

> Yes, that's important. And it would be great if they offered language classes.

2. Your next-door neighbors moved out, and your apartment manager told you that new neighbors are going to move in next week. Express your hopes about the new neighbors. For example, you can talk about who the neighbors will be, what kind of neighbors they will be, or what kind of relationship you will have with them.

3. You and your group members are going on a camping vacation in a national park. You've never gone camping before. Express your hopes for the trip. For example, you can talk about the weather, the campground, the activities available, and animals you might encounter.

# Grammar

## Using Past Modals to Make Inferences

We use *must have* and *can't have* to make inferences from evidence. Use *must have* + past participle to infer that something was almost certainly true or almost certainly happened.

> It **must have been** incredibly difficult for the Ikoma people to leave the Serengeti.

Use *can't have* + past participle to infer that something was unbelievable or nearly impossible.

> Well, it's their land, so they **can't have felt** happy about being asked to move again.

**Making Inferences.** With a partner, read the scenarios. Then answer the questions by making inferences with *must have* and *can't have*.

1. Researchers have found that Native Americans' DNA links them to people living in southern Siberia. The DNA does not link them with Europeans. Where did the Native Americans originally migrate to the Americas from?
2. Researchers have been unable to find any Neanderthal DNA in studies of modern humans, although they know that Neanderthals lived in Europe and Asia when modern humans first came there. What happened to the Neanderthals?
3. The oyamel tree of Mexico is the favorite habitat of the monarch butterfly. Three trees were found on the ground in the Mexican Monarch Butterfly Reserve. Logging is illegal there, and logging companies are careful to obey the law. What happened to the oyamel trees?
4. A large group of wildebeest suddenly stopped grazing and began running as fast as possible. Why did the wildebeest suddenly start running?

These two Dutch artists created this sculpture of a Neanderthal woman.

Your group is going to do a research project about a migrating animal. Then you will give a presentation to the class with the information you found.

 **A | Getting Background Information.** Form a group with two or three other students. Discuss the answers to the following general questions about migration:

- Why do animals migrate?
- What are some types of migration?
- How do animals know when to migrate?
- How do animals know where to go?

**B | Researching.** Select a migrating animal that you will present to the class. Find a photo of the animal and print it out. Do not choose an animal that you learned about in this unit. On your own, research the animal. When you research the animal, follow these steps:

1. Look for information on the Internet, or in newspapers, books, and encyclopedias.
2. Choose relevant key words to help you narrow down your search.
3. Make sure the information is accurate and reliable. (*See page 212 of the Independent Student Handbook for more information on researching.*)

**C | Organizing Information.** Use the chart to take notes about the animal you selected. Then discuss your notes with your group members. Did you all find similar information?

| | |
|---|---|
| **Name of Animal** | |
| **Size of Animal** | |
| **Habitat** | |
| **Lifespan (Length of Life)** | |
| **Geographic Range** | |
| **Distance Traveled** | |
| **Time of Migration** | |
| **Reason for Migration** | |
| **Description of the Migration** | |
| **Other Interesting Points** | |

**D | Presentation.** Organize your notes and practice your presentation. Then present the information to the class. Answer any questions from your audience.

**Presentation Skills: Preparing for Audience Questions**

Questions from the audience are part of most presentations, so it's a good idea to be prepared for them. As part of your preparation, spend some time thinking about the kinds of questions that your audience might ask you. Then think about how you will answer.

# Overview

The *Independent Student Handbook* is a resource that you can use at different points and in different ways during this course. You may want to read the entire handbook at the beginning of the class as an introduction to the skills and strategies you will develop and practice throughout the book. Reading it at the beginning will provide you with another organizational framework for understanding the material.

Use the *Independent Student Handbook* throughout the course in the following ways:

**Additional instruction:** You can use the *Independent Student Handbook* to provide more instruction on a particular skill that you are practicing in the units. In addition to putting all the skills instruction in one place, the *Independent Student Handbook* includes additional suggestions and strategies. For example, if you find you're having difficulty following academic lectures, you can refer to the Improving Your Listening Skills section to review signal phrases that help you to understand the speaker's flow of ideas.

**Independent work:** You can use the *Independent Student Handbook* to help you when you are working on your own. For example, if you want to improve your vocabulary, you can follow some of the suggestions in the Building Your Vocabulary section.

**Source of specific tools:** A third way to use the handbook is as a source of specific tools such as outlines, graphic organizers, and checklists. For example, if you are preparing a presentation, you might want to use the Research Checklist as you research your topic. Then you might want to complete the Presentation Outline to organize your information. Finally, you might want to use the Presentation Checklist to help you prepare for your presentation.

## Table of Contents

# Formal Listening Skills

## Predicting

Speakers giving formal talks or lectures usually begin by introducing themselves and then introducing their topic. Listen carefully to the introduction of the topic and try to anticipate what you will hear.

*Strategies:*

- Use visual information including titles on the board, on slides, or in a PowerPoint presentation.
- Think about what you already know about the topic.
- Ask yourself questions that you think the speaker might answer.
- Listen for specific phrases.

### Identifying the Topic:

*Let's look at . . .*
*Today's topic is . . .*
*What I want to do today is . . .*
*Today, we're going to cover . . .*

## Understanding the Structure of the Presentation

An organized speaker will use certain expressions to alert you to the important information that will follow. Notice the signal words and phrases that tell you how the presentation is organized and the relationship between the main ideas.

*Introduction*

A good introduction includes a thesis statement, which identifies the topic and gives an idea of how the lecture or presentation will be organized.

### Introduction (Topic + Organization):

*I'd like to focus on . . .*　　　　　*To begin with . . .*
*There are basically two groups . . .*　　*There are three reasons . . .*
*Several factors contribute to this . . .*　*There are five steps in this process . . .*

*Body*

In the body of the lecture, the speaker will usually expand upon the topic presented in the introduction. The speaker will use phrases that tell you the order of events or subtopics and their relationship to each other. For example, the speaker may discuss several examples or reasons.

### Following the Flow of Ideas in the Body:

*However, . . .*　　　　　　　　*As a result, . . .*
*For example, . . .*　　　　　　　*Let's move on to . . .*
*The first/next/final (point) is . . .*　　*Another reason is . . .*

*Conclusion*

In a conclusion, the speaker often summarizes what has already been said and may discuss implications or suggest future developments. For example, if a speaker is talking about an environmental problem, he or she may end by suggesting what might happen if we don't solve the problem, or he or she might add his or her own opinion. Sometimes speakers ask a question in the conclusion to get the audience to think more about the topic.

**Restating/Concluding:**

*In summary, . . .*                    *To sum up, . . .*
*As you can see, . . .*                *In conclusion, . . .*


## Listening for Main Ideas

It's important to distinguish between a speaker's main ideas and the supporting details. In school, a professor often will test a student's understanding of the main points more than of specific details. Often a speaker has one main idea just like a writer does, and several main points that support the main idea.

*Strategies:*

- Listen for a thesis statement at the end of the introduction.
- Listen for rhetorical questions, or questions that the speaker asks, and then answers. Often the answer is the thesis.
- Notice ideas that are repeated or rephrased.

**Repetition/Rephrasing:**

*I'll say this again . . .*                    *So again, let me repeat . . .*
*Let me put it another way . . .*             *The most important thing to know is . . .*
*What you need to know is . . .*


## Listening for Details (Examples)

A speaker will often provide examples that support a main point. A good example can help you understand and remember the main point.

*Strategies:*

- Listen for specific phrases that introduce an example.
- Notice if an example comes after a generalization the speaker has given, or is leading into a generalization.
- If there are several examples, decide if they all support the same idea or are different aspects of the idea.

**Giving Examples:**

*. . . such as . . .*                         *. . . including . . .*
*The first example is . . .*                  *For instance, . . .*
*Here's an example of what I mean . . .*      *Let me give you an example . . .*

## Listening for Details (Reasons)

Speakers often give reasons, or list causes and/or effects to support their ideas.

*Strategies:*

- Notice nouns that might signal causes/reasons (e.g., *factors, influences, causes, reasons*), or effects (e.g., *effects, results, outcomes, consequences*).
- Notice verbs that might signal causes/reasons (e.g., *contribute to, affect, influence, determine, produce, result in*) or effects (often these are passive, e.g., *is affected by*).
- Listen for specific phrases that introduce reasons/causes.

### Giving Reasons:

*This is because . . .*                          *This is due to . . .*
*The first reason is . . .*                       *In the first place . . .*

### Giving Effects or Results:

*As a result, . . .*                              *Therefore, . . .*
*Consequently, . . .*                             *One consequence is . . .*
*Another effect is . . .*

## Understanding Meaning from Context

Speakers may use words that are unfamiliar to you, or you may not understand exactly what they've said. In these situations, you can guess the meaning of a particular word or fill in the gaps of what you've understood by using the context or situation itself.

*Strategies:*

- Don't panic. You don't always understand every word of what a speaker says in your first language either.
- Use context clues to fill in the blanks. What did you understand just before or just after the missing part? What did the speaker probably say?
- Listen for words and phrases that signal a definition or explanation.

### Giving Definitions:

*Or . . .*                                        *In other words, . . .*
*. . . meaning that . . .*                        *That is (to say), . . .*
*(By which) I mean . . .*                         *To put it another way . . .*

## Recognizing a Speaker's Bias

Speakers often have an opinion about the topic they are discussing. It's important for you to understand if they are objective or subjective about the topic. Being subjective means having a bias or a strong feeling about something. Objective speakers do not express an opinion.

*Strategies:*

- Notice words such as adjectives, adverbs, and modals that the speaker uses (e.g., *ideal, horribly, should, shouldn't*).
- Listen to the speaker's voice. Does he or she sound excited, happy, or bored?
- When presenting another point of view on the topic, is that given much less time and attention by the speaker?
- Listen for words that signal opinions.

### Opinions:

*If you ask me, . . .*          *In my opinion, . . .*
*(Personally,) I think . . .*      *As far as I'm concerned . . .*

## Making Inferences

Sometimes a speaker doesn't state something directly, but instead implies it. When you draw a conclusion about something that is not directly stated, you make an inference. For example, if the speaker says he or she grew up in Spain, you might infer that he or she speaks Spanish. When you make inferences, you may be very sure about your conclusions or you may be less sure. It's important to use information the speaker states directly to support your inferences.

*Strategies:*

- Note information that provides support for your inference. For example, you might note that the speaker lived in Spain.
- Note information that contradicts your inference. Which evidence is stronger—for or against your inference?
- If you're less than certain about your inference, use words to soften your language such as modals, adverbs, and quantifiers.

*She probably speaks Spanish, and she **may** also prefer Spanish food. **Many** people from Spain are familiar with bullfighting.*

## Summarizing or Condensing

When taking notes, you should write down only the most important ideas of the lecture. To take good notes quickly:

- Write only the key words.

  *dusky seaside sparrow extinct*

- You don't need complete sentences.

  *~~That's why the~~ Endangered Species Act, ~~which was~~ passed in the United States in 1973, protects ~~both~~ endangered animals and ~~their~~ habitats*

- Use abbreviations (short forms) and symbols when possible.

  | | | | |
  |---|---|---|---|
  | *info* information | *dr* doctor | *w/* with | < less than |
  | *ex.* examples | *b/c* because | = /→ leads to causes | > more than |

## Outlining

Another way to take clear and organized notes is to use an outline. Like with other types of note-taking, in an outline you should only write key ideas and you should use abbreviations and symbols when possible. To indicate main ideas in an outline, use Roman numerals (I, II, III) and capital letters (A, B, C). Indicate details with numbers. As information becomes more specific, move it to the right.

    I. Background

       A. 1970s & 1980s: Soviet Union developed nuclear technology

       B. 1986: 25 plants w/ safety probs.

    II. Chernobyl disaster

       A. Causes

          1. Mistakes during safety test

          2. No containment building to limit fire and radiation

       B. Result: explosion → people dead

## Recognizing Organization

When you listen to a speaker, you practice the skill of noticing that speaker's organization. As you get in the habit of recognizing the organizational structure, you can use it to structure your notes in a similar way. Review the signal words and phrases from the Improving Your Listening Skills section in this handbook.

Some basic organizational structures are:

- Narrative (often used in history or literature)
- Process (almost any field, but especially in the sciences)
- Cause and Effect (history, psychology, sociology)
- Classification (any field, including art, music, literature, sciences, history)
- Problem and Solution

## Using Graphic Organizers

Graphic organizers can be very useful tools if you want to rewrite your notes. Once you've identified the speaker's organizational structure, you can choose the best graphic organizer to show the ideas. See the Resources section on page 214 in this handbook for more information.

## Distinguishing between Relevant and Irrelevant Information

Remember that not everything a speaker says is noteworthy. A lecturer or presenter will usually signal important information you should take notes on.

### Signals for Important Information:

*Don't forget that . . .*

*It is important to note/remember that . . .*

*Let me stress that . . .*

*You need to remember that . . .*

Instructors and other lecturers may also signal when to stop taking notes.

### Signals to Stop Taking Notes:

*You can find this in your handout . . .*

*You don't have to write all this down . . .*

*This won't be on your test . . .*

*This information is in your book . . .*

In a similar way, they may let you know when they are going to discuss something off-topic.

### Understanding Sidetracks:

*That reminds me . . .*

*On a different topic . . .*

*This is off the subject, but . . .*

*Incidentally . . .*

*As an aside . . .*

*By the way, . . .*

## Recognizing a Return to a Previous Topic

When a speaker makes a sidetrack and talks about something that is not directly related to the main topic, he or she will often signal a return to a previous topic.

### Returning to a Previous Topic:

*Back to . . .*

*To continue . . .*

*So, just to restate . . .*

*OK, so to get back on topic . . .*

*Getting back to what we were saying . . .*

*To return to what we were talking about earlier . . .*

## Using Notes Effectively

It's important to not only take good notes, but also to use them in the most effective way.

*Strategies:*

- Go over your notes after class to review and add information you might have forgotten to write down.
- Compare notes with a classmate or study group to make sure you have all the important information.
- Review your notes before the next class, so you will understand and remember the information better.

# Independent Vocabulary Learning Tips

**Keep a vocabulary journal.**

- If a new word is useful, write it in a special notebook. Also write a short definition (in English if possible) and the sentence or situation where you found the word (its context). Write your own sentence that uses the word.
- Carry your vocabulary notebook with you at all times. Review the words whenever you have free time.
- Choose vocabulary words that will be useful to you. Some words are rarely used.

**Experiment with new vocabulary.**

- Think about new vocabulary in different ways. For example, look at all the words in your vocabulary journal and make a list of only the verbs. Or, list the words according to the number of syllables (one-syllable words, two-syllable words, and so on).
- Use new vocabulary to write a poem, a story, or an email message to a friend.
- Use an online dictionary to listen to the sound of new words. If possible, make a list of words that rhyme. Brainstorm words that relate to a single topic that begin with the same sound (*student, study, school, skills, strategies, studious*).

**Use new words as often as possible.**

- You will not know a new vocabulary word after hearing or reading it once. You need to remember the word several times before it enters your long-term memory.
- The way you use an English word—in which situations and with what other words—might be different from a similar word in your first language. If you use your new vocabulary often, you're more likely to discover the correct way to use it.

**Use vocabulary organizers.**

- Label pictures.

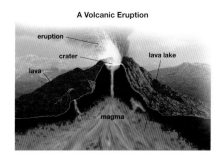

A Volcanic Eruption

- Make word maps.

- Make personal flashcards. Write the words you want to learn on one side. Write the definition and/or an example sentence on the other.

# Prefixes and Suffixes

Use prefixes and suffixes to guess the meaning of unfamiliar words and to expand your vocabulary. Prefixes usually change the meaning of a word somewhat. Suffixes usually change the part of speech. If you train yourself to look for the base meaning, or the meaning of the stem of the word, you can understand more vocabulary.

| Prefix | Meaning | Example |
|--------|---------|---------|
| a- | completely; not | awake; apolitical |
| bi- | two | bilingual, bicycle |
| dis- | not, negation, removal | disappear, disadvantages |
| pre- | before | prehistoric, preheat |
| mis- | bad, badly, incorrectly | misunderstand, misjudge |
| re- | again | remove |
| un- | not, the opposite of | unhappy, unusual, unbelievable |

The following are derivational suffixes that change the part of speech of the base word.

| Suffix | New Part of Speech | Example |
|--------|--------------------|---------|
| -able | adjective | believable |
| -ary | noun | summary |
| -ent | adjective | convergent, divergent |
| -ful | adjective | beautiful, successful |
| -ed | adjective | stressed, interested |
| -ize | verb | summarize |
| -ly | adverb | carefully, completely |
| -ment | noun | assignment |
| -tion | noun | information |

# Dictionary Skills

The dictionary listing for a word usually provides the pronunciation, part of speech, other word forms, synonyms, examples of sentences that show the word in context, and common collocations.

## Synonyms

A *synonym* is a word that means the same thing (e.g., *baby=infant*). Use synonyms to expand your vocabulary.

## Word Families

These are the words that have the same stem or base word, but have different prefixes or suffixes.

## Different Meanings of the Same Word

Many words have several meanings and several parts of speech. The example sentences in the word's dictionary entry can help you determine which meaning you need. For example, the word *plant* can be a noun or a verb.

## Collocations

Dictionary entries often provide *collocations*, or words that are often used with the target word. For example, if you look up the word *get*, you might see *get around, get into, get there*, and so on.

# Everyday Communication

## Summary of Useful Phrases for Everyday Communication

It's important to practice speaking English every day, with your teacher, your classmates, and anyone else you can find to practice with. This chart lists common phrases you can use in everyday communication situations. The phrases are listed in this chart from more formal to less formal.

| | |
|---|---|
| **Asking for Clarification:** | **Digressing from the Topic:** |
| *Could you explain . . . (for me, please)?* | *Speaking of . . .* |
| *What do you mean by . . . ?* | *That reminds me, . . .* |
| *What (exactly) is . . . ?* | *Incidentally . . .* |
| *(Sorry,) what does . . . mean?* | *By the way . . .* |
| **Agreeing:** | **Expressing Hopes:** |
| *I agree.* | *It would be nice/great/wonderful/ideal if . . .* |
| *I think so too.* | *I'm hoping (that) . . .* |
| *I think you're right.* | *I (really) hope (that) . . .* |
| *Exactly!* | |
| *You can say that again!* | |
| **Disagreeing:** | **Apologizing for Interrupting:** |
| *I disagree.* | *I'm sorry. I didn't mean to cut you off.* |
| *I'm not so sure (about that) . . .* | *What were you going to say?* |
| *That's debatable.* | *Go ahead.* |
| *I don't think so.* | *Sorry.* |
| *That's crazy!* | |
| *No way!* | |
| **Conceding a Point:** | **Asking Sensitive Questions:** |
| *Good point.* | *Excuse me for asking, but . . . ?* |
| *Fair enough.* | *Do you mind if I ask you . . . ?* |
| *I'll give you that.* | *If you don't mind my asking, . . .?* |
| **Expressing Surprise:** | **Congratulating the Group:** |
| *That's amazing/astonishing/incredible.* | *Nice job, everybody!* |
| *That's (really) surprising.* | *Congratulations!* |
| *Wow!* | *We make a great team!* |
| *No kidding.* | *Great going, gang!* |
| *Imagine that!* | *Good for you!* |
| | *Way to go, guys!* |
| **Expressing Encouragement:** | **Expressing Interest:** |
| *Good luck!* | *Is that so?* |
| *Go for it!* | *How interesting!* |
| *Go get 'em!* | *I didn't know that.* |

| Expressing Approval and Disapproval: | Joining a Group: |
|---|---|
| *(I) think it's fine to . . .* | *Do you mind if I join your group?* |
| *It's OK that . . .* | *Do you want to work together?* |
| *It's not right for (someone) to . . .* | *Do you need another person?* |
| *It's wrong to . . .* | |
| **Enumerating:** | **Checking Background Knowledge:** |
| *First, . . . Second, . . . Third, . . .* | *Do you know about . . . ?* |
| *First . . . , then . . . , and then . . .* | *Have you (ever) heard of . . . ?* |
| *For one thing, . . . For another, . . .* | *What do you know about . . . ?* |
| *And for another, . . .* | *What can you tell me about . . . ?* |

## Doing Group Projects

You will often have to work with a group on activities and projects. It can be helpful to assign group members certain roles. You should try to switch roles every time you do a new activity. Here is a description of some common roles used in group activities and projects:

**Group Leader**—Makes sure the assignment is done correctly and all group members participate. Asks questions: *What do you think? Does anyone have another idea?*

**Secretary**—Takes notes on the group's ideas (including a plan for sharing the work).

**Manager**—During the planning and practice phases, the manager makes sure the presentation can be given within the time limit. If possible, practice the presentation from beginning to end and time it.

**Expert**—Understands the topic well; invites and answers audience questions after the presentation. Make a list of possible questions ahead of time to be prepared.

**Coach**—Reminds group members to perform their assigned roles in the group work.

Note that group members have one of these roles in addition to their contribution to the presentation content and delivery.

## Classroom Presentation Skills

### Library Research

If you can go to a public library or school library, start there. You don't have to read whole books. Parts of books, magazines, newspapers, and even videos are all possible sources of information. A librarian can help you find both print and online sources of information.

## Online Research

The Internet is a source with a lot of information, but it has to be looked at carefully. Many Web sites are commercial and may have incomplete, inaccurate, or biased information.

### Finding reliable sources

*Strategies:*

• Your sources of information need to be reliable. Think about the author and the publisher. Ask yourself: *What is their point of view? Can I trust this information?*

• Your sources need to be well respected. For example, an article from *The Lancet* (a journal of medical news) will probably be more respected than an article from a popular magazine.

• Start with Web sites with *.edu* or *.org* endings. These are usually educational or non-commercial Web sites. Some *.com* Web sites also have good information, for example www.nationalgeographic.com or www.britannica.com.

### Finding information that is appropriate for your topic

*Strategies:*

• Look for up-to-date information, especially in fields that change often such as technology or business. For Internet sources, look for recent updates to the Web sites.

• Most of the time, you'll need to find more than one source of information. Find sources that are long enough to contain some good information, but not so long that you won't have time to read them.

• Think about the source's audience. For example, imagine that you are buying a new computer and want to read about the different types of computers before you buy one. If the source is written for computer programmers, for example, you might not be able to understand it. If the source is written for university students who need to buy a new computer, it's more likely to be understandable.

## Speaking Clearly and Comprehensibly

It's important that your audience understands what you are saying for your presentation to be effective.

*Strategies:*

• Practice your presentation many times for at least one other person and ask him or her for feedback.

• Make sure you know the correct pronunciation of every word—especially the ones you will say more than once. Look them up online or ask your instructor for the correct pronunciation.

• Try to use thought groups. Keep these words together: long subjects, verbs and objects, clauses, prepositional phrases. Remember to pause slightly at all punctuation and between thought groups.

• Speak loudly enough so that everyone can hear.

• Stop occasionally to ask your audience if they can hear you and follow what you are saying.

## Demonstrating Knowledge of Content

You should know more about your subject than you actually say in your presentation. Your audience may have questions or you may need to explain something in more detail than you planned. Knowing a lot about your subject will allow you to present well and feel more confident.

*Strategies:*

- Practice your presentation several times.
- Don't read your notes.
- Say more than is on your visuals.
- Tell your audience what the visuals mean.

### Phrases to Talk about Visuals:

*You can see . . .*
*The main point is that . . .*
*The line/box represents . . .*
*This graph/diagram shows/explains . . .*

## Engaging the Audience

Presenting is an important skill. If your audience isn't interested in what you have to say, then your message is lost.

*Strategies:*

- Introduce yourself.
- Make eye contact. Look around at different people in the audience.
- Use good posture. *Posture* means how you hold your body. When you speak in front of the class, you should stand up straight. Hold your hands together in front of your waist, if you aren't holding notes. This shows that you are confident and well prepared.
- Pause to check understanding. When you present ideas, it's important to find out if your audience understands you. Look at the faces of people in the audience. Do they look confused? Use the expressions from the chart below to check understanding.

### Phrases to Check for Understanding:

*OK so far?*
*Are you with me?*
*Have you got that?*
*Does that make sense?*
*Do you have any questions?*

# Understanding and Using Visuals: Graphic Organizers

## T-Chart
**Purpose:** Compare or contrast two things or list aspects of two things

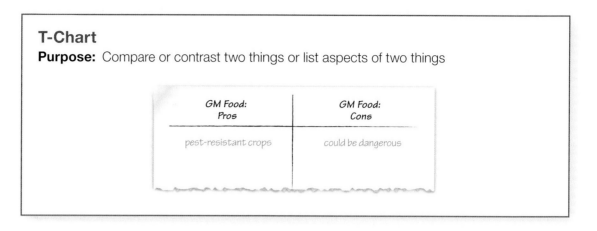

## Venn Diagram
**Purpose:** Show differences and similarities between two things, sometimes three

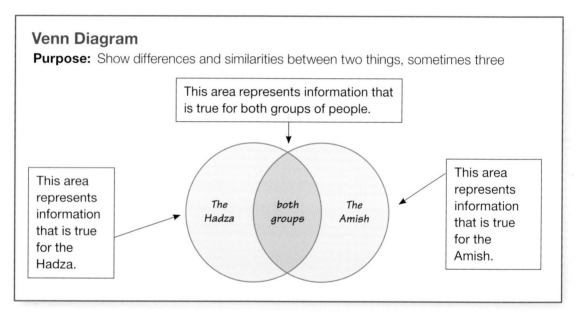

## Family Tree
**Purpose:** Organize information about your family relationships

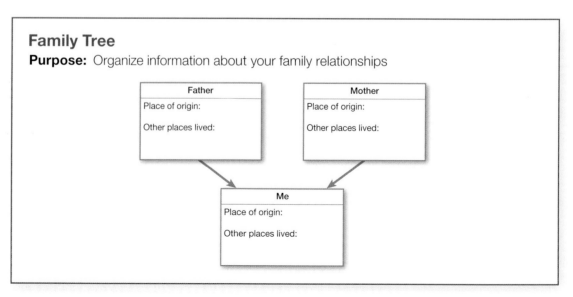

## Flow Chart

**Purpose:** Show the stages in a process, or a cause-and-effect chain (Flow charts have many different shapes.)

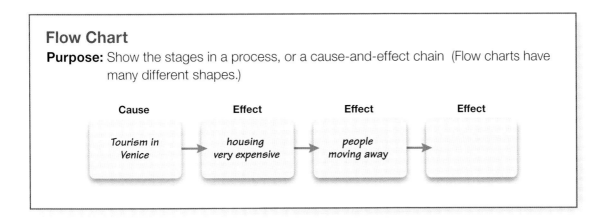

## Timeline

**Purpose:** Show the order of events and when they happened in time

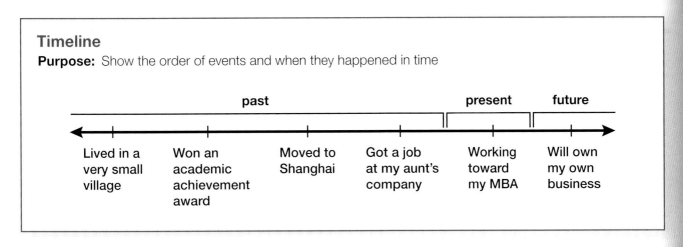

## Idea Map

**Purpose:** Brainstorm ideas or identify main points or themes of a listening or reading. (A Spider Map can also be used for this purpose.)

# Understanding and Using Visuals: Maps, Charts, Graphs, and Diagrams

**Maps** are used to show geographical information.

The **key** or **legend** explains specific information about the map. This legend shows the location of France in relation to nearby continents.

The **labels** on a map show important places mentioned in a reading or listening passage.

**Bar** and **line graphs** use axes to show the relationship between two or more things.

**Bar graphs** compare amounts and numbers.

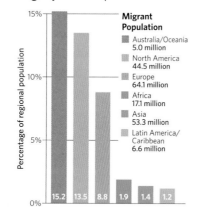

**Migrant Population**
- Australia/Oceania 5.0 million
- North America 44.5 million
- Europe 64.1 million
- Africa 17.1 million
- Asia 53.3 million
- Latin America/Caribbean 6.6 million

The **y axis** shows the percentage of foreign immigrants in Germany.

**Line graphs** show a change over time.

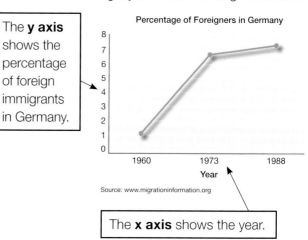

Source: www.migrationinformation.org

The **x axis** shows the year.

**Pie charts** show percents of a whole, or something that is made up of several parts.

## Fossil Fuel Use by Sector

This section shows that the Energy Supply sector uses the most fossil fuels.

- Waste and Wastewater 3%
- Energy Supply 26%
- Transportation 13%
- Forestry 17%
- Agriculture 14%
- Industry 19%
- Residential and Commercial Buildings 8%

**Diagrams** are a helpful way to show how a process or system works.

reservoir
dam
power station
turbine

# Presentation Outline

When you are planning a presentation, you may find it helpful to use an outline. If it is a group presentation, the outline can provide an easy way to divide the content. For example, someone could do the introduction, another student the first main idea in the body, and so on.

I. **Introduction**

Topic: _____

_____

Hook/attention getter: _____

_____

Thesis statement: _____

_____

II. **Body**

A. First step/example/reason: _____

Supporting details:

1. _____
2. _____
3. _____

B. Second step/example/reason: _____

Supporting details:

1. _____
2. _____
3. _____

C. Third step/example/reason: _____

Supporting details:

1. _____
2. _____
3. _____

III. **Conclusion**

Major points to summarize: _____

_____

Any implications/suggestions/predictions: _____

_____

Closing comment/summary: _____

_____

# Checklists

## Research Checklist

- ☐ Do I have three to five sources for information in general—and especially for information I'm using without a specific citation?
- ☐ Am I correctly citing information when it comes from just one or two sources?
- ☐ Have I noted all sources properly, including page numbers?
- ☐ When I am not citing a source directly, am I using adequate paraphrasing? (a combination of synonyms, different word forms, and/or different grammatical structure)
- ☐ Are my sources reliable?

## Presentation Checklist

- ☐ Have I practiced several times?
- ☐ Did I get feedback from a peer?
- ☐ Have I timed the presentation?
- ☐ Do I introduce myself?
- ☐ Do I maintain eye contact?
- ☐ Do I explain my visuals?
- ☐ Do I pause sometimes and check for understanding?
- ☐ Do I use correct pronunciation?
- ☐ Do I have good posture?
- ☐ Am I using appropriate voice volume so that everyone can hear?

## Pair and Group Work Checklist

- ☐ Do I make eye contact with others?
- ☐ Do I pay attention when someone else is talking?
- ☐ Do I make encouraging comments?
- ☐ Do I ask for clarification when I don't understand something?
- ☐ Do I check for understanding?
- ☐ Do I clarify what I mean?
- ☐ Do I express agreement and disagreement politely?
- ☐ Do I make suggestions when helpful?
- ☐ Do I participate as much as my classmates?
- ☐ Do I ask my classmates for their ideas?

# Summary of Signal Phrases

**Giving Recommendations:**
*It's (probably) a good idea (not) to . . .*
*It might be wise (not) to . . .*
*If I were you, I wouldn't . . .*
*Have you thought about . . .?*

**Showing Understanding:**
*You must be (tired).*
*You must have been (glad).*
*That must be (fun).*
*That must have been (difficult).*

**Using Fillers:**
*Let me think*
*Just a moment*
*Oh, what's the word . . .*
*. . . um . . .*
*. . . hang on . . .*

**Expressing Uncertainty:**
*It appears/looks/seems as though . . .*
*It appears/seems to me (that) . . .*
*I'm not quite/altogether sure (that) . . .*
*I could be wrong, but it appears/doesn't*
*    appear (that) . . .*

**Paraphrasing:**
*I mean . . .*
*In other words . . .*
*That is (to say) . . .*
*Let me put it another way . . .*
*To put it another way . . .*

**Enumerating Reasons and Examples:**
*First, Second, Third . . .*
*First, Next, After that . . .*
*First, Then, And then . . .*
*For one thing, For another, And for*
*    another . . .*
*In the first place, In the second place,*
*    And in the third place . . .*

**Expressing a Lack of Knowledge:**
*I had no idea (that) . . .*
*I didn't realize (that) . . .*
*I never knew (that) . . .*
*I wasn't aware (that) . . .*

**Giving Effects or Results:**
*As a result, . . .*
*One consequence is . . .*
*Consequently . . .*
*Therefore, . . .*
*Another effect is . . .*

**Giving Definitions:**
*. . . which means . . .*
*In other words, . . .*
*What that means is . . .*
*Another way to say that is . . .*
*That is . . .*

**Expressing Opinions:**
*As far as I'm concerned, . . .*
*In my opinion, . . .*
*(Personally,) I think . . .*
*If you ask me, . . .*
*As I see it, . . .*

**Signal to Stop Taking Notes:**
*You don't have to write all this down . . .*
*This information is in your book . . .*
*You can find this in your handout . . .*
*This won't be on your test . . .*

**Returning to a Previous Topic:**
*So, just to restate . . .*
*Back to . . .*
*Getting back to what we were saying . . .*
*To return to what we were talking about*
*    earlier . . .*
*OK, so to get back on topic . . .*

**Understanding Sidetracks:**
*That reminds me . . .*
*By the way . . .*
*This is off the subject, but . . .*
*As an aside . . .*
*On a different topic . . .*

**Confirming Understanding:**
*Are you following me?*
*Does that make sense?*
*Have you got that?*
*Any questions?*
*Are you with me?*
*OK so far?*

*These words are on the Academic Word List (AWL). The AWL is a list of the 570 highest-frequency academic word families that regularly appear in academic texts. The AWL was compiled by researcher Averil Coxhead based on her analysis of a 3.5 million word corpus (Coxhead, 200).

# Critical Thinking

# Grammar

# Language Function. *See also* Grammar; Pronunciation; Speaking

# Test-Taking Skills

categorizing, 8, 40

checking correct answers, 17, 37, 73, 77

circling correct answers, 96

fill in blanks, 5, 8, 14, 16, 18, 25, 28, 35, 38, 45, 48, 54, 55, 58, 59, 65, 68, 70, 72, 78, 79, 88, 95, 98

matching, 4, 12, 14, 24, 32, 34, 44, 46, 52, 64, 74, 84, 85, 87, 92

multiple choice, 6, 7, 27, 47, 53, 67, 73, 86

sentence completion, 9, 10, 13, 15, 29, 30, 39, 55, 79

sequencing, 53, 93

short answers, 6, 59

true/false questions, 15, 16, 75, 76, 96

# Topics

Beauty and Appearance, 41–60

Energy Issues, 61–80

Migration, 81–100

Protecting Our Planet, 21–40

Urban Challenges, 1–20

# Viewing

and collaboration, 32

and critical thinking, 13, 53, 73, 93

*Crocodiles of Sri Lanka*, 32-33

for main idea ideas, 13, 52, 73

for specific details, 13

and note-taking, 32, 93

and predicting content, 12, 32, 52

and sequencing events, 53, 93

*Skin Mask*, 52-53

*Solar Power*, 72-73

*Tuareg Farmers*, 12-13

using a dictionary, 12, 32, 52, 92

visuals/graphic organizer

    diagrams 72

    maps, 92

*Wildebeest Migration*, 92-93

# Vocabulary

building vocabulary, 4, 14, 24, 34, 44, 54, 64, 74, 84, 94

    dictionary use, 4, 5, 12, 14, 15, 25, 32, 34, 52, 54, 55, 66, 85, 92, 209

    experimenting with new vocabulary, 208

    keeping a vocabulary journal, 208

    meaning from context, 4, 24, 34, 44, 64, 74, 84

    prefixes, 209

    suffixes, 55, 209

    using new words as often as possible, 208

    vocabulary organizers, 208

using vocabulary, 5, 15, 25, 35, 45, 55, 65, 75, 85, 95

    choosing the right definition, 85

    dictionary use, 5, 15, 25, 55, 85

# Writing

cartoon captions, 7

combining sentences, 30, 39

conversations, 10

in charts, 15, 31, 91

notes for presentations, 60

note-taking, 26, 27, 33, 36, 87, 93, 206

    researching for presentations, 80

    using a graphic organizer, 76

    using an outline, 66, 67, 206

questions, 57

sentences, 29

Spider Map, 20